THE CALIFORNIA LAND

THE CALIFORNIA
LAND
PLANNING
FOR PEOPLE

The Report of the
California Land-Use Task Force

y the Planning and Conservation Foundation
William Kaufmann, Inc.

The work of the California Land-Use Task Force and the preparation of this report were made possible by a grant from the Michael J. Connell Foundation of Los Angeles.

Library of Congreess Cataloging in Publication Data

California Lane-Use Task Force.
  The California land.

  A companion volume, by Sedway/Cooke, was published simultaneously under title: Land and the environment.
  Includes index.
  1. California—Environmental policy. 2. Regional planning—California. I. Planning and Conservation Foundation. II. Title.
HC107.C23E557 1975   333.7'09794   75-19439
ISBN 0-913232-20-3

Printed in the United States of America by Banta West.
Composition by Holmes Composition Service.
Cover by Gabriele von Rabenau.
Design by John Beyer.

CONTENTS

Preface	6
Summary of Recommendations	8
Introduction	9
Chapter One	
Land-Use Planning Agencies	13
Chapter Two	
Issues and Findings	31
1. CITIES	33
2. HOUSING	39
3. AGRICULTURE	47
4. RESOURCES	55
5. ENERGY	61
6. TRANSPORTATION	67
7. TAXATION	73
8. COMPENSATION	77
Chapter Three	
RECOMMENDATIONS	83
Appendix	90
Picture Credits	94
Index	95

PREFACE

This report is the result of twelve months of study and debate by the California Land-Use Task Force.

In it we set forth a plan of action for dealing with the complex problem of land-use planning in California.

It is addressed to Governor Edmund G. Brown, Jr. and his Administration; to the members of the California State Legislature; to elected local officials; and to the people of California.

In preparing this report we have looked closely at how and where decisions which affect the use of land are made.

We have concluded that the lack of comprehensive land-use planning is a major impediment to the kind of future we want for California. It lies at the root of many of California's major problems, environmental, social, and economic. It demands our serious attention, and the work must begin immediately.

The Land-Use Task Force was organized and funded by the California Planning and Conservation Foundation. The task force membership is evenly divided between the leadership of the California business community and the major public interest organizations concerned with land-use problems.

The task force began with the conviction that an orderly process which assures the wise use of land is indispensable for the future of California: that for business as for labor, for the conservationist as for the developer, there is much to be gained from an overhaul of the complex, haphazard methods by which California governments now control, or seek to control, the use of land.

Over the course of the year, the Task Force has held twenty full day working sessions. There have been many meetings of its smaller working groups. Its members have travelled many thousands of miles and considered literally thousands of pages of information and drafts. It has heard and questioned speakers of imposing reputation and experience, among them:

Gilbert Finnell, author of the Florida Planning Act, one of the first major steps toward state wide land-use planning in any state;

Alfred Heller, editor of *The California Tomorrow Plan,* a blueprint for the future of the land and society of California;

William K. Reilly, Executive Director of the Rockefeller Brothers Fund Task Force on Land-use and Urban Growth and editor of its report, *The Use of Land;*

Thomas P. Gill, former Lieutenant Governor of Hawaii, and principal architect of Hawaii's unique system of state wide zones;

Fred Bosselman, one of the nation's most prominent land-use attorneys and co-author of *The Quiet Revolution in Land-use Control* and *The Taking Issue;*

The Honorable **Gerald Talmadge Horton,** member of the House of Representatives of the State of Georgia and a national authority on land-use planning.

The Task Force also met with Donald W. Benedict, Principal Program Analyst of the California Legislative Analyst's office; with Professor Donald G. Hagman, Professor of Law at UCLA and director of an ongoing study of compensation techniques; and with Law Professor Ira Michael Heyman, Vice-Chancellor of the University of California, Berkeley.

The California Land-Use Task Force came together with the conviction that land use was of common concern to the many divergent interest groups within the state: that it should be possible for representatives of these groups to sit down together to explore problems, clear away misunderstandings and arrive at some fundamental points of agreement on what steps California should take toward comprehensive land-use planning.

Our report is a consensus document resulting from an attempt to accommodate different points of view. There were, of course, many issues on which we disagreed. But the refreshing discovery—which made the entire experience valuable and productive—was that there were more areas of agreement than disagreement.

Therefore, we believe that the conclusions of this report are both solid and encouraging. We believe that the new methods suggested here will work and that they are seriously needed. We urge that they be enacted into law. We recommend them to you.

This report is divided into three chapters. Chapter One is a brief overview of the various governmental agencies which now have authority—direct or indirect—over land use in California. Chapter Two is a survey of eight key subject areas related to land-use planning, with specific policy findings on each. Chapter Three presents our recommendations for a new comprehensive state land-use planning process.

SUMMARY OF RECOMMENDATIONS

NEEDED ACTION: Comprehensive planning must be a top priority of the new Administration and the new Legislature. The Legislature should begin the creation of a statewide land-use planning process in 1975.

GOALS: Land-use planning to preserve the quality of the environment and provide for orderly development; land-use legislation which integrates environmental, social and economic policies.

DIVISION OF RESPONSIBILITIES: State planning decisions only on matters of state-wide importance. Area-wide planning for regional problems within the framework of state guidelines. Local planning within the framework of state and regional guidelines.

LAND-USE COUNCIL: A State Land-Use Council should be created by the Legislature in 1975 to coordinate all state planning and develop a comprehensive state land-use plan.

Structure: Five full-time members, appointed by the Governor and confirmed by the Senate; the Chairman to serve as a Secretary of Cabinet rank. A 15-member citizens' advisory group.

Functions: Prepare state land-use plan, enforce interim legislative land-use policies, coordinate planning and projects of state agencies and departments, review annual state budget for accordance with land-use policies, and maintain statewide data bank.

Guidelines: Legislature to establish policies and guidelines regarding agriculture, urban growth, resource protection, housing, energy efficiency and urban revitalization.

Land-Use Plan: To be developed and submitted to the Legislature in 1977. To contain: identification of land in various categories relative to agriculture, urbanization and resources; recommendations for their protection or development; implementation program; policies for achieving noise, water and air quality standards; designation of regions for area-wide planning agencies; strategy for urban revitalization; taxation and compensation policies; recommendation for modification of governmental structures; recommended procedures for adherence to standards of due process.

Other Agencies: Council to absorb the Office of Planning and Research and the Council on Intergovernmental Relations; to review projects and programs of all other state agencies and resolve conflicts between them; to review federal policies affecting land-use.

AREA-WIDE PLANNING: State Land-Use Plan to delineate regions for area-wide planning. Each region to have a planning council charged with developing a comprehensive regional plan and authorized to resolve land-use conflicts among local jurisdictions.

LOCAL GOVERNMENT: Most planning decisions should continue to be made at the local level within the framework of state and area-wide plans.

INTRODUCTION

Of all the great issues before us today, land use may be the least understood. Yet land is the basic resource, and in one way or another all of the problems which the human race must confront in this century—problems of food, housing, energy, resources, population—lead us to the central question of how the land is used.

Land use cannot be labelled as merely an "environmental" issue. It is far broader than that. It is a fundamental human activity which affects every business person, worker, and consumer.

In the past Californians have taken an interest in land-use problems, but they have only looked at some small part of the over-all picture: at the need for open space, the problems of power plant siting, or the preservation of a unique natural resource, for example. And they have responded with single-purpose programs. There is little evidence, so far, of any understanding that these many land-use problems and their resolution tie in with one another and depend on one another—that they are, in fact, different aspects of the same problem.

It is time to take a look at the whole picture, and to begin to create a comprehensive process for deciding how the land of California is to be used. Failure to do so would be a tragedy for present and future generations.

Already there are alarming signs that the land is in danger: that many of the natural qualities that have brought people to California, made it such a rich and productive part of the Earth, are deteriorating.

- California's farmland is being converted to urban uses without thought for the future needs of the state.
- While suburbs expand across vacant lands, older downtown areas are rapidly declining.
- At the same time, the housing shortage—especially for people of low and moderate income—increases.
- Air pollution continues to cause severe damage to humans and crops.
- Our store of natural resources dwindles rapidly, unable to keep up with ever growing demands.

Meanwhile, the energies of business people, developers, conservationists and elected officials have been absorbed in wasteful disputes over particular land-use issues. Decisions are often years in coming and rarely satisfactory to all concerned.

Land-Use in California

In order to fully understand the California planning process, it is necessary to know how California's land is now being used, who owns the land, and how many people the land must support.

A look at existing land-use patterns reveals that agriculture, California's leading industry, uses approximately 36 percent of the land. And the great majority of 20 million citizens live on only two percent of the land—mainly near the coast.

CALIFORNIA LAND USE*

Class of land	Number of acres	Percent of State's Area
Total	100,185,000	100.0
Forest Land	42,416,000	42.3
Commercial[a]	17,345,000	17.3
Public	9,253,000	9.2
Private	8,092,000	8.1
Productive-Reserved[b]	1,255,000	1.3
Unproductive[c]	23,816,000	23.8
Agricultural	35,722,000	35.7
Cropland[d]	11,815,000	11.8
Urban and suburban land[e]	2,200,000	2.2
Other land[f]	19,847,000	19.8

[a]Forest land producing or capable of producing crops of industrial wood and not withdrawn from timber utilization by statute or administrative regulation.

[b]Productive public forest land withdrawn from timber utilization through statute or administrative regulation.

[c]Forest land incapable of yielding crops of industrial wood because of adverse site conditions.

[d]As reported by 1964 Census of Agriculture. Excludes land cultivated in developing improved pasture.

[e]Residential areas containing at least five homes, with a density of one home or more on each two acres; industrial and commercial development; and the actively occupied portions of military reservations—as determined by land and water use specialists of the Department of Water Resources.

[f]Consists mainly of publicly owned open space.

*Source: Department of Finance, *California Statistical Abstract,* 1970.

In counties which have absorbed most of the state's increasing population, many of California's rich agricultural lands have been converted to urban use. In other counties, new lands have been brought into production. Since a higher and higher proportion of new housing is built in low-density suburbs, the degree of conversion of agricultural lands will continue to rise—unless the energy shortage or other factors discourage low-density development.

Statistics from the U. S. Census Bureau show the combined total of prime agricultural lands and newly irrigated lands in California counties.

TOTAL ACRES IRRIGATED*

County	1954	1964	1969
Alameda	22,599	24,227	17,788
Alpine	2,118	2,692	no data
Amador	1,290	3,815	5,495
Butte	161,628	170,433	177,490
Calaveras	5,580	4,393	5,144

County	1954	1964	1969
Colusa	138,929	163,606	171,754
Contra Costa	50,117	56,407	38,793
Del Norte	2,833	4,494	3,476
El Dorado	7,008	5,796	8,539
Fresno	905,433	1,060,314	1,045,173
Glenn	136,511	151,298	148,295
Humboldt	18,027	19,184	19,175
Imperial	418,682	429,594	450,216
Inyo	29,674	19,552	26,921
Kern	569,293	603,659	680,719
Kings	416,787	436,037	351,135
Lake	12,498	15,322	19,744
Lassen	53,018	61,991	76,132
Los Angeles	147,288	78,813	65,078
Madera	193,804	212,052	209,974
Marin	974	688	500
Mariposa	3,083	1,305	3,097
Mendocino	13,246	14,614	16,069
Merced	336,542	377,817	349,955
Modoc	124,772	133,759	149,903
Mono	20,402	11,386	17,520
Monterey	148,941	177,906	174,765
Napa	8,390	10,909	8,169
Nevada	10,530	7,797	3,613
Orange	101,140	54,893	34,076
Placer	43,415	28,571	23,104
Plumas	22,001	31,320	21,362
Riverside	194,997	228,673	178,841
Sacramento	147,150	169,237	127,514
San Benito	31,770	38,820	33,414
San Bernardino	101,981	81,173	53,260
San Diego	62,779	52,436	56,083
San Francisco	-0-	-0-	-0-
San Joaquin	430,565	496,948	447,544
San Luis Obispo	26,634	30,357	41,484
San Mateo	6,623	5,517	7,107
Santa Barbara	68,984	65,079	62,635
Santa Clara	114,677	78,665	63,889
Santa Cruz	17,982	23,175	16,007
Shasta	44,961	56,797	43,478
Sierra	14,201	10,741	5,692
Siskiyou	93,552	113,788	121,639
Solano	79,971	112,355	105,790
Sonoma	20,231	27,985	22,397
Stanislaus	336,755	349,694	306,866
Sutter	192,534	195,572	201,138
Tehama	50,766	72,613	72,138
Trinity	3,664	2,432	1,052
Tulare	535,500	585,361	554,622
Tuolumne	3,885	2,272	3,621
Ventura	112,306	103,161	91,928
Yolo	172,218	252,184	232,169
Yuba	56,810	68,981	67,259
State Total	7,048,049	7,598,698	7,240,131

*U.S. Department of Commerce, Census Bureau, United States Census of Agriculture.

Land Ownership

The federal government owns about half of the land in California—a fact which obviously has a great deal to do with California land use. About 95 percent of federal lands in California are under the management of the U.S. Forest Service and the Bureau of Land Management. These two agencies between them control half of the state's commercial forest acreage (though much less than half of the most productive forest land). The Department of Defense holds most of the remaining five percent of federal land.

LAND OWNERSHIP IN CALIFORNIA *

Government Owned	Acres	% area
Total	50,335,945	50.2
Federal	45,251,036	45.2
Indian Land	540,473	.54
State	2,437,809	2.4
Counties	691,827	.69
Cities	865,895	.86
School Districts	80,025	.08
Jr. College Districts	7,012	.01
Special Districts	461,868	.46
Privately Owned	49,847,735	49.8

*Source: State Lands Commission: "Public Land Ownership in California, 1973"

Population

The 1970 census counted almost 20 million people in California. More than 16 million of them—80.1 percent—live in and around major cities, in what the Bureau of Census calls "urbanized areas." Sixty percent of the state's population lives in the eight southern counties. Los Angeles County alone contains nearly a third of the people in the state.

Growth in the 1960's was not evenly distributed. Southern California added people much faster than the north, and the greatest growth, north or south, was on the suburban fringe. Overall, the state's population increased 27 per cent between 1960 and 1970—while the suburban population more than doubled. There has been little new community development in remote rural areas, but many second-home land subdivisions.

Although rates of growth have declined slightly, the California population continues to increase. The California State Department of Finance forecasts a population in excess of 30 million by the year 1995—half again as many people as were living here in 1970.

Given these population pressures, it is becoming more and more clear that our patched and improvised set of rules for deciding land-use questions is inadequate. They need critical examination. New demands for space, resources, energy and public services will crowd in upon us even as we struggle to learn from and rectify the deficiencies and weaknesses of earlier land-use policies. Whether we welcome this growth or not, we must take responsibility for it and work out explicit and coherent policies for doing business on—and with—the land.

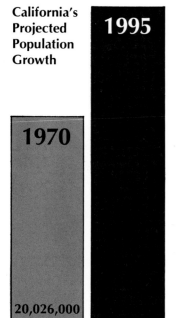

California's Projected Population Growth

1995

1970

20,026,000

Source: State Dept. of Finance

Chapter One

LAND-USE PLANNING AGENCIES

Since the basic theme of this report is the need for a unified process of land-use planning in California, it seems reasonable to ask whether land use is not being planned and controlled already.

And indeed it is: By some 1400 local governments. By special districts. By regional agencies. By departments of state government. By agencies of the federal government. The decisions are made in literally thousands of different places. More planning is being done in California today than ever before. It may even be true that there is more good planning than ever before, but this still does not add up to a comprehensive planning process.

There are cases of inter-agency "coordination," but in fact planning in California is not coordinated. Some plans do not fit with other plans, some controls do not match other controls, some controls are not based upon plans at all. Sometimes one agency does the work of another, and sometimes one undoes the work of another. There are many pieces to the picture; but they do not add up to a single whole that landowners, business interests, public officials and citizen groups can relate to with the secure knowledge that it represents California land-use policy.

We do not believe that the development of such a policy must always result in more controls. In some cases it should result in less. However, it is important that controls be related to better, more considered and more explicit purpose.

In this chapter, as a first step toward determining how such a policy might evolve, we briefly review existing governmental structures for land use planning: state, regional and local.[1] Since our aim is the creation of a state planning process, we do not deal here with federal agencies—but it must be kept in mind that the federal government exerts a powerful influence on California land use. It is the largest single landowner in California. Its laws on air and water quality have forced the state to strengthen its own controls. Its funds play a part in any major planning, construction, or preservation project.

The federal presence will have to be considered in the development of state land-use policy and, conversely, state initiatives in this area could become a model for future national land-use policies.

---

[1] This chapter is a condensation of *Land and the Environment: Planning in California Today* prepared by Sedway/Cooke, San Francisco for The Planning and Conservation Foundation. Copies may be obtained from William Kaufmann, Inc., One First Street, Los Altos, Ca. 94022.

CALIFORNIA LAND-USE

A. STATE LEVEL PLANNING

1. State Comprehensive Planning Agencies

a. Office of Planning and Research

b. Council on Intergovernmental Relations

2. State Development Planning Agencies

a. Department of Transportation

b. Department of Housing

c. Public Works Board

3. State Resource Planning Agencies

a. Air Resources Board
b. State Water Resources Control Board
c. California Coastal Zone Conservation Commission
d. Energy Resources Conservation and Development Commission
e. Department of Fish and Game
f. Department of Parks and Recreation
g. Department of Water Resources
h. Department of Navigation and Ocean Development
i. Solid Waste Management Board
j. University of California

4. Related Regulatory Agencies

a. State Lands Commission

b. Public Utilities Commission

PLANNING AGENCIES

B. REGIONAL LEVEL PLANNING

1. Councils of Government

2. Statutory Regional Agencies

a. Metropolitan Transportation Commission
b. Bay Conservation and Development Commission
c. Tahoe Regional Planning Agency

C. LOCAL LEVEL PLANNING

1. The Local General Plan

2. Implementation of the General Plan

a. Zoning
b. Subdivision Regulation
c. Urban Renewal
d. Housing
e. Growth Management
f. Property Taxation
g. Environmental Impact Assessment
h. Local Agency Formation Commissions
i. Airport Land Use Commissions

A. STATE LEVEL PLANNING

There are four types of state agencies involved in land-use planning: (1) comprehensive planning agencies; (2) development planning agencies; (3) resources planning agencies; and (4) related regulatory agencies.

1. State Comprehensive Planning Agencies

The Office of Planning and Research (OPR) and the Council on Intergovernmental Relations (CIR) have been combined within the Governor's Office. CIR is an internal division of OPR with only a handful of staff personnel and a comparable budget and political mandate. OPR has a somewhat larger staff, budget and potentially significant statutory mandate. Even without major new statutory powers, OPR/CIR could take a leading part in defining (but not implementing) state and substate land-use policies. This would require more adequate funding and a clear mandate from the Governor.

Office of Planning and Research

The Office of Planning and Research is the state agency responsible for comprehensive land-use and environmental policy planning. Actually it has no direct power over land use, and is a weak planning agency given to inter-agency coordination, and unenforceable "paper plans."

A recent study of OPR, by both OPR and the federal Department of Housing and Urban Development, concluded that there is, in fact, little comprehensive planning at the state level. OPR functions primarily as the research staff of the Governor and Cabinet. State funding for OPR is low: indeed, most of its studies are financed by federal grants.

The HUD study ascribed OPR's weakness partly to a bias against state planning. State planning has been equated with state control of land use and zoning. The strong home rule tradition favoring decentralized, local planning, has prevailed.

Council on Intergovernmental Relations

The Council on Intergovernmental Relations is an advisory body composed of 22 members appointed by the Governor. Its main responsibility is the development of guidelines to assist local agencies in the preparation of city and county general plans. The guidelines are advisory only. Each city and county must annually report the degree to which its adopted general plan complies with CIR's guidelines, but the reports are not legally self-incriminating against a non-compliant local government.

Sometimes, however, it appears that the guidelines are taken too seriously by local planners and tend to frustrate or divert the local planning process. In field interviews with local planners, four principal criticisms emerged: (1) Many planning departments lacked staff or budgets to meet deadlines or prepare plan elements of adequate quality. (2) The technical requirements of the guidelines either were not intelligible or were over-articulated for some elements (e.g., noise) and under-articulated for others (e.g., housing). (3) Some of the guidelines are simply not relevant to local conditions. (4) The degree of local compliance with the guidelines is not reviewable by a state or regional planning agency. The nearest approximation to a review process is the environmental impact report (EIR) which must accompany each new local general plan or plan element.

The proliferation of guidelines, moreover, is being interpreted by some local planners as an implicit state policy of requiring local governments to solve state or regional level problems. Adequate planning for many needs transcends the authority and scale of local governments: housing for low and moderate (and perhaps, middle) income families is more a regional problem, while planning for open space preservation frequently necessitates regional and statewide approaches.

2. State Development Planning Agencies

In the absence of explicit state level planning it was inevitable that a de facto planning process would emerge. Some state agencies develop public works projects which have massive land-use consequences.

Department of Transportation (Caltrans)

The planning and administration of California's varied transportation programs are in the hands of the Department of Transportation—Caltrans—newly reconstituted under a 1972 law aimed at: (1) deemphasis of road construction in favor of balance between highway and mass transit systems; (2) development of a statewide comprehensive Transportation Plan by 1976; and (3) development of the State Transportation Plan through a "bottoms up" planning process relying on substate transportation plans based upon local general plans.

The actual financing and implementation of mass transit systems was reserved to local governments. Thus, implementation powers for highways and freeways remain at the state level, while implementation of mass transit systems is the responsibility of local government.

Caltrans is actually the institutional successor to the

former Department of Public Works, which was mainly concerned with a single transportation mode—highways and freeways. The district offices of the Division of Highways are now under the direct supervision of the Director of Transportation and their staffs have been enlarged to perform multi-modal transportation planning in cooperation with local and regional transportation planning agencies (TPA's).

The state Department of Transportation was directed to prepare the California Transportation Plan for achieving "a coordinated and balanced" statewide transportation system. The Plan is to include mass transit, highway, aviation, maritime and railroad systems and is to be "consistent with the state's social, economic, and environmental needs and goals."

But mere enactment of a new planning law did not in itself insure a new planning process. Caltrans absorbed more than 15,000 personnel from the former Department of Public Works. Many are highway engineers who, although undergoing retraining in multimodal systems, work for an organization which—like its predecessor—is limited to implementing highways and freeways. Implementing mass transit systems requires technical and political skills foreign to the experience of most Caltrans personnel.

The law does not satisfactorily address the relationship of new highway and freeway projects to land-use patterns, nor to state and federal air quality standards. It provides no well-defined or enforceable air quality standards to ensure that new highway projects, the State Transportation Plan or the state/substate planning process are effectively regulated. It also provides for no more than "consideration" of air quality impacts, and after two years of review of Caltrans projects, the Air Resources Board (ARB) found that this consideration was often inadequate.

Department of Housing and Community Development

The Department of Housing and Community Development and its governing body, the Commission of Housing and Community Development, are authorized: (1) to act as an information source for housing and community development programs; (2) to protect and conserve the large equities that the majority of California residents have now accumulated in single family homes; and (3) to improve housing conditions of the state's farmworkers.

The commission establishes departmental policy. The Department assists local governments and private enterprise on community development and housing matters. It is also responsible for coordinating federal-state relationships in housing and encouraging full utilization of federal programs.

As a "facilitating" type of agency, the Department has had minor influence upon housing and land-use related planning in the state. It is statutorily weak, with nominal powers and budget.

State Public Works Board

The State Public Works Board reviews construction projects funded by the Legislature and must approve land acquisitions by all state agencies except the Department of Transportation, Department of Water Resources, Reclamation Board, University of California and community colleges. It must also approve sales of surplus state property authorized by the Legislature.

Although the Board cannot make policy, it can veto or modify projects proposed by the Legislature and other state agencies.

3. State Resource Planning Agencies

Air Resources Board

In California the relationship between state and substate air pollution control agencies roughly parallels the federal/state model. The stationary source powers of the local agencies predated creation of the state level Air Resources Board, and today the state government generally plays a supervisory role only. But state level enforcement powers have been expanding recently, principally in response to federal air quality requirements.

At the county level, the board of supervisors is also the board of the Air Pollution Control District (APCD). APCD's have primary responsibility for controlling stationary sources. The only regional APCD is the Bay Area Air Pollution Control District comprised of the nine Bay Area counties and governed by a board having representatives of both cities and counties.

In response to federal law requiring establishment of a single state agency for air pollution control, the Mulford-Carrell Air Resources Act of 1967 created the state's Air Resources Board. It directly administers the state's program for control of motor vehicle emissions and oversees regional stationary source control.

The ARB has five principal sets of air pollution control responsibilities.

● To divide the state into air basins.
    To date, the basin-wide approach has not

proven an effective planning or regulatory unit, because the formation of basin-wide boards is not mandatory, and has been resisted by most counties.

- To promulgate ambient air quality standards for each air basin.
- To promulgate rules and regulations.
- To promulgate emission standards for all stationary and other non-vehicular sources for each basin.

While the ARB is responsible for adopting stationary standards, the county APCDs may adopt more stringent standards. However, if the ARB determines that an APCD program cannot achieve and maintain ambient standards, it may assume the powers of the APCD and enforce the state's emission standards.

- To develop test procedures to measure compliance with state stationary emission standards.

Land Use and Transportation Controls

Issuance of permits for new sources of emissions is the primary responsibility of county APCDs, which must operate within ARB-approved basin implementation plans.

These state regulations have significant land-use implications. A new stationary source may be forbidden if its emissions contribute to pollutant concentrations exceeding an ambient standard, even though it cannot be proven that the source by itself would violate the standard. The regulations in effect subdivide the air basin into pollutant concentration areas. In areas of low pollution concentrations, new sources probably will be approved; where concentration levels are high, it is more likely that they will be denied. The regulations may induce new stationary sources to locate in cleaner areas in order to secure the required permit.

The Environmental Protection Agency's proposed regulations for indirect stationary sources would require urban area APCDs to incorporate indirect source controls into their pollution programs. This would involve approval or denial of new highways, airports, shopping centers, amusement parks, and other major vehicle-related land developments.

While the ARB initially pioneered the use of vehicle exhaust controls, its position regarding land-use and transportation controls has been merely reactive to federal initiatives and requirements. The ARB has stated that it does not want to be the state agency making basic land-use decisions. Any state level intrusion into local land-use control is, according to a former ARB official, "a hot potato."

The ARB has never found it necessary to take direct regulatory action in any local control district. Rather, its activities have been restricted to preparing reports on major stationary sources, preparing emission inventories, suggesting additional regulations, and investigating citizen complaints.

Although an inter-agency agreement between ARB and Caltrans provides for "coordinating" transportation planning with air pollution control, it does not per se ensure development of effective Transportation Control Plans (TCPs) for California's five critical air basins. An effective TCP should include strategies for reducing automobile usage.

ARB's environmental review of new Caltrans projects, including proposed freeway development in critical air basins, is activated after the fact—i.e., after Caltrans has already made the basic decision to undertake the project. The most ARB can do is to slow down project development by challenging the environmental analysis contained in the EIR. It can not challenge a decision by Caltrans that a new freeway is "needed" even where the ambient air quality of an urban basin already exceeds permissible national limits.

State Water Resources Control Board

Water pollution control and its relationship to land-use development patterns is similar to the air quality/land use interaction. The 1972 federal Water Pollution Control Act seeks the complete elimination of all pollution discharges by 1985. The law requires secondary treatment of all waste water by July 1977.

California's water pollution control program predated the federal program and served as a model for some of its provisions. While most states were concentrating on developing standards for receiving waters, California began controlling the sources of pollution and instituted a waste discharge system. California also required regional water quality plans, a strategy reflected in the federal act's requirements for a continuing areawide planning process and implementation plan. The state program continues to be more extensive than the federal.

The State Water Resources Control Board (SWRCB) is the state level agency designated for water pollution control. It is authorized to formulate a state water quality policy, integrating resource planning with pollution control. Because regional boards and other state agencies are required to comply with water quality policy, SWRCB is able to influence the activities of other state agencies such as highway and park development.

Other responsibilities of SWRCB include administering the research program for water pollution control, coordinating water quality investigations and formulating planning procedures for the regional boards to follow in developing their regional water quality control plans. SWRCB's supervision over the preparation of 16 basin plans prepared by nine regional boards has resulted in a coherent and effective planning process.

Regional water quality control boards administer and enforce waste treatment systems. Decisions of the regional boards may be appealed to the state board. All meetings of the state and regional boards are open to the the public—and public participation is invited. The regional boards are authorized to enforce their discharge requirements through cease and desist orders, and through clean-up and other remedial orders.

Grant Programs

The State Water Resources Control Board also administers state and federal grants for the planning and construction of sewage treatment plants. The board reviews applications for grants, determines their conformity with state regional water quality plans and certifies that the project is entitled to ranking.

Coastal Zone Conservation Commissions

The Coastal Zone Conservation Act was approved by California voters as Proposition 20, in November 1972. The Act is intended to protect the California coast by "a comprehensive, coordinated, enforceable plan for orderly, long-range conservation and management" prepared by the State Coastal Zone Conservation Commission and six regional commissions.

The main duties of the commissions are preparing the Coastal Zone Conservation Plan and administering the interim permit system. The regional commissions are active participants in preparation of the plan. Each must prepare its recommendations and submit them to the state commission, which must then adopt a state coastal plan and submit it to the Legislature in December 1975.

While the plan is being prepared, the act vests strong interim regulatory powers in the state and regional commissions. Any development begun after February, 1973 within the "permit area" must be approved by a regional commission. The permit area does not include the entire coastal zone. It extends seaward three miles as does the coastal zone, and inland to 1,000 yards from the mean high tide mark. The coastal zone extends inland to the highest peak of the coastal range,

or five miles—whichever distance is smaller.

All lands under the jurisdiction of the San Francisco Bay Conservation and Development Commission are specifically excluded from the permit area. Any urban land developed and stabilized to a residential density of four or more dwelling units per acre by January 1972, and commercial or industrial land stabilized before that date, may also be excluded.

The fact that the permit area does not cover the entire coastal zone has been criticized because development of inland sections of the coastal zone could significantly affect coastal resources. If the act had included the entire coastal zone the Commissions could better guide development of all lands while the plan is being prepared. On the other hand, the administrative burden of reviewing every new development within the entire coastal zone would probably have been overwhelming.

State Energy Resources
Conservation and Development Commission

This is a new state-level planning and regulatory agency created by legislation in 1974 with authority to plan for electrical energy needs within the state and to certify new thermal electrical generation facilities.

The Commission has exclusive authority over standards (except air and water quality standards) for new generation facilities. It can preempt all other standards previously applied by other state agencies and local governments. Multiple permit proceedings before such agencies as local planning commissions, local legislatures and the Public Utilities Commission have been replaced by a single proceeding before the new Energy Commission. It is primarily responsible for the preparation of the environmental impact report which must accompany any application to construct a new thermal electric generating facility.

The Commission is charged with assessing trends in energy use, adopting effective energy conservation measures, and determining long- and short-term energy needs. It is directed to set new building and design standards and to prepare guidelines for evaluating the energy efficiency of new residential, commercial and industrial structures.

The Commission has nearly exclusive power to certify new electric generating sites and related facilities. Other state agencies and local governments make recommendations to the Commission; hearings are held; comment is made on otherwise applicable local plans and standards; the Commission shall require an EIR to be prepared. The Commissions's siting authority is not entirely exclusive: a permit from the Coastal Zone Conservation Commission is still required; air and water standards adopted by other agencies are applicable; and the Legislature has listed a number of areas of critical environmental concern (e.g., parks) where new facilities would be barred.

Department of Fish and Game

The Department of Fish and Game is within the Resources Agency. A five member Fish and Game Commission assists with policy direction. It is authorized to regulate the taking or possession of birds, mammals, fish, amphibians and reptiles except for commercial purposes, to promulgate rules and regulations relating to the state's fish and wildlife. It is empowered, among other things, to review and approve proposed projects involving the acquisition of land and water for ecological reserves.

The Department may establish ecological reserves and acquire property for conservation purposes. Under various programs, it now owns approximately 120,000 acres and is responsible for carrying out construction projects on property acquired under the Wildlife Conservation Act. However, it has little influence on state land-use planning decisions. Its planning is most direct and significant for those areas sheltering endangered or rare species, including habitats.

Department of Parks and Recreation

The Department of Parks and Recreation is an executive department within the Resources Agency, and operates under policies set by the Parks and Recreation Commission.

The Department has broad powers for administering, developing, planning and operating park and recreation facilities in the state. It may acquire or lease property so as to enhance and maintain the state's outdoor recreation resources and coordinates state and local agencies having an interest in planning, developing, and maintaining these resources. It designs, constructs, operates and maintains recreational facilities at state water projects, and manages the land and water surfaces of such projects for recreational purposes.

The Department is one of the state agencies which have a major impact on the state's land-use planning decisions. It is the lead agency in developing and maintaining statewide recreation plans and also influences

local land-use decisions through its operating policies and relations with local governments. Public recreation resources often encourage private development, notably second home subdivisions and retail trade.

Department of Water Resources

The Department of Water Resources (DWR) is probably best known for the State Water Project and Aqueduct and the California Water Plan, undertakings related to its primary functions of conservation, development and transportation of the state's water resources. Located within the Resources Agency, the Department is the product of a wide ranging reorganization and consolidation in 1956 of the state's water resource activities. The State Reclamation Board is part of the Department and is now in the process of being consolidated with it.

a. Departmental Organization

The Department is under the control of a director appointed by the Governor, subject to Senate confirmation. Exercise of the Department's rule-making (regulatory) power is divided between the director and California Water Commission, a nine-member body having general policy-making powers except as described below. The state Reclamation Board cooperates with the U.S. Army Corps of Engineers in planning and constructing flood control projects on the Sacramento and San Joaquin rivers and their tributaries.

b. Principal Planning Powers
(1) California Water Plan

After the conclusion of World War II, the state in the late 1940's undertook studies leading toward a long-range plan for comprehensive development of water resources. The eventual result was the California Water Plan, adopted in 1959, which was to serve as "the guide for the orderly and coordinated control, protection, conservation, development, and utilization of the water resources of the State," and may be amended as needed by the Legislature and Department.

The State Water Project was also approved in 1959, with the Legislature authorizing a $1.75 billion state bond issue to finance system construction. The bond issue was approved by the voters in 1960; revised estimates place total Project costs at approximately $3 billion.

(2) Water Exportation

In order for the Legislature to determine the availability of water supplies for export from the watersheds of their origination, the Department is instructed to conduct investigations and hearings and to report its findings to the Legislature. The investigations are to determine watershed boundaries and the quantity of water originating therein; the quantity of water "reasonably required for ultimate beneficial use" in the watersheds; the amount of water, if any, available for export from the watersheds; and areas of the state "which can be served by the water available for export from each watershed."

(3) Multiple Use Planning

The Department is to undertake planning for public recreation uses and fish and wildlife preservation as part of its general project development activities for water facilities. The legislative purpose is to provide for multiple use of state water storage, conservation and recreation facilities, and for the planning and acquisition of real property concurrently with land acquisition for water facilities.

(4) Ground Water Basin Protection

A significant portion of the state's water is stored, distributed and furnished by ground water basins that are subject to overdraft, depletion, saline intrusion and pollution. To prevent degradation or irreparable damage to such basins, the Legislature intended, "whenever money is appropriated for the purpose," that the Department undertake investigations, studies, plans and design criteria for construction of projects deemed "to be practical, economically feasible and urgently needed."

Department of Navigation and Ocean Development

The Department of Navigation and Ocean Development is primarily responsible for those ocean-oriented activities of state government not otherwise subject to the jurisdiction of the Coastal Zone Conservation Commission, including the coordination of marina and small harbor development and beach erosion control. Its planning functions have been largely superseded by the various state and regional coastal plans currently in progress.

Solid Waste Management Board

The State Solid Waste Management Board (SWMB), essentially a single-purpose planning agency, was created by the Legislature in 1974 and charged with initiation of statewide solid waste management policy, a research and development program, and related information and research activities. Its jurisdiction was explicitly circumscribed by a legislative policy enunciating "that the primary responsibility for adequate solid waste management and planning shall rest with local government."

The Solid Waste Management Board consists of seven voting members, compensated at the rate of $100 per day for attending meetings, and is located within the Resources Agency. The Board is assisted by a 25-member, noncompensated advisory body known as the State Solid Waste Management and Recovery Advisory Council.

State Policy for Solid Waste Management

The state board was required to adopt by January 1975, and thereafter periodically review and revise, the State Policy for Solid Waste Management.The Policy is to include "minimum standards" for solid waste handling and disposal "for the protection of air, water, and land from pollution." Although the state standards "may include" the location, design, operation, maintenance and ultimate reuse of solid waste processing, and disposal facilities, they "shall not include" those aspects which are "solely of local concern . . . such as, but not limited to, frequency of collections, means of collection and transportation, level of service, charges and fees, designation of territory served through franchises, contracts, or governmental services, and purely aesthetic considerations."

Substate Solid Waste Management Plans

The state Board was instructed to provide guidelines and necessary technical assistance for the preparation of substate solid waste plans. Each county, "in cooperation with affected local jurisdictions," must prepare a solid waste management plan, that is "comprehensive, coordinated and consistent with" the State Policy as well as any regional or sub-regional solid waste plans. Alternatively, a regional planning agency recognized by the state Council on Intergovernmental Relations (typically a Council of Governments or statutory regional agency) may prepare the plan if authorized by the county and a majority of the cities within the county which have a majority of the incorporated area population.

University of California

In 1965, the Regents of the University of California established the Natural Land and Water Reserves System to provide a series of natural reserves encompassing the diversity of California's natural habitats, both aquatic and terrestrial, for teaching and research use.

The system now consists of twenty reserves, containing a total of 74,265 acres. In addition to originally granted university lands, reserves have been acquired by direct purchase, by gift and by use of lease agreements with federal, state, and local agencies.

The use of reserve lands is restricted to field studies and ecological research by university students or other authorized persons.

4. Related Regulatory Agencies

State Lands Commission

The State Lands Commission has exclusive responsibility for administering state public lands, including vacant school lands, tidelands, submerged lands, swamp and overflowed lands, and beds of navigable rivers and lakes. It has statutory power to sell, lease, or dispose of land under its jurisdiction, provided that the transaction is in "the public interest," and is authorized to approve or disapprove permits for the private use of state lands, such as offshore oil drilling in submerged lands within state jurisdiction. It has broad power to exchange state tidelands and submerged lands for publicly or privately owned lands.

Because of this power, the Commission has significant influence over land-use planning and growth patterns in some areas of the state. For example, there are approximately 287,000 acres of undeveloped state "school" lands in San Bernardino County; if sold to private developers, they could have considerable effect on land-use patterns, growth rates, service availability, environmental quality and land economics in the area. Another example is the leasing of tidal and submerged lands for offshore oil drilling, which has significant consequences for environmental quality, shoreline land uses and related land economics. The approval of sale or granting of a lease by the Commission in either case, would have major land-use effects but would not be guided by a comprehensive planning process which identifies alternatives and evaluates their respective impacts.

Public Utilities Commission

The Public Utilities Commission regulates the services and rates of privately owned utilities and transportation companies, although publicly-owned utilities are not under its jurisdiction. Its authority includes licensing utility facilities; certification of plant construction or expansion and high voltage transmission; and review of power plant siting. (Primary authority over the siting of electrical facilities has been transferred to the new Energy Resources Conservation and Development Commission.)

Utilities and transportation services affect the type and location of growth, and have considerable impact on local environments. Thus, the PUC in making its decisions is performing a powerful de facto land-use planning role.

B. REGIONAL LEVEL PLANNING

Planning at the regional level is performed by (1) Councils of Governments and (2) statutory regional planning agencies.

1. Councils of Governments

Three different California statutes enable local governments to create regional planning organizations. However, two of them—the District Planning Law and the Regional Planning District Law—have never been implemented; a third, the Area Planning Law, has been used only rarely. The more successful regional organi-

zations, such as the Association of Bay Area Governments (ABAG) and the Southern California Association of Governments (SCAG), have been created under another law, the Joint Exercise of Powers Act. In all these instances the state has merely enabled local governments to act together: it has not mandated such action or created a regional planning authority.

The Joint Exercise of Powers Act, first adopted in 1949, sets forth very general provisions which regulate agreements among cities, among cities and counties, and even among local governments and state and federal agencies. The functions which may be performed under such agreements are extremely diverse, but do not include the exercise of police power. Thousands of intergovernmental contracts are in existence in California, allowing cooperation in providing public services such as hospitals, sewage facilities, and police protection. Many of the activities performed under such agreements involve land use: construction of local flood control projects, maintenance of open space as parks and provision of utility services. Joint powers agreements have formed the basis for a large number of government associations currently exercising planning functions. These voluntary arrangements are referred to as Councils of Governments (COGs).

The earliest associations of governments in California were formed in the metropolitan areas of San Francisco, Southern California, and Sacramento. Each of the COGs included five or more counties as members. COGs in other areas of the state were created later and are usually based in only one county. Because these non-metropolitan COGs were formed in response to federal legislation, their initial responsibilities were highway planning and open space. At present, the major functions of "single-county" COGs are (1) review of grant applications, (2) areawide planning, and (3) provision of technical assistance to member jurisdictions.

Although these associations have the power under state statute to formulate regional policies, their only enforcement power is derived from the federal government. COGs are certified by the federal Office of Management and Budget to act as regional clearing houses, reviewing federal (A-95) grant applications by local agencies to determine whether the applications conform to the regional plan.

A recent study of seven "single-county" COGs indicates that the review process is not effectively used at present. The substantive comments made on grant applications are rarely helpful, rarely desired, and the review is mere "rubber stamp." There are several reasons for this: most applications are not seen by the COGs as being of sufficient area-wide significance to require substantive comment between levels of government. Moreover, it is very difficult to assess area-wide significance when an application is considered without reference to a comprehensive area plan. In many COGs, there is not yet a plan of sufficient detail or scope to make a meaningful review. In addition, local officials are hesitant to be critical of the applications of other jurisdictions, and expect the same support for their own projects. The failure of federal and state government to require consistent compliance with grant requirements

is another reason COGs have not emphasized the review process.

The primary rationale for the existence of COGs is their potential role as area-wide planning bodies. Actually, however, area-wide planning has largely been in response to federal and state requirements, such as transportation planning and specially funded studies. Even when planning is undertaken at the COG level, it is rarely direct planning, but rather an effort at "coordination" of the activities of local city and county planners. The underlying problems are the absence of a well-defined planning role in a region where other planning agencies are better-established and a reliance on "consensus decision-making."

SCAG

The Southern California Association of Governments, formed in 1965, is the largest COG in California. It is engaged in programs which effect more than ten million people in its 38,000 square mile region. Nearly 80 percent of all municipalities in the area are members.

In 1973, SCAG began a technical assistance program to provide planning aid to communities of under 50,000 residents. It is the designated clearinghouse for federal grant reviews and environmental impact reviews, commenting on thousands of projects. After several years effort, a Regional Airport System Plan was adopted by SCAG as the first completed element of an overall transportation plan. Also in 1973, planning goals and policies were approved. Together with previously existing general guidelines and new regional growth forecasts, the goals and policies comprise the Southern California Development Guide, which is intended to serve as the reference point for all of SCAG's functions. At present, the grant and environmental impact reviews are the primary tools for implementing area-wide objectives. Even in these areas, however, SCAG's comments are advisory only.

ABAG

In 1961, the first COG in California was formed in the San Francisco Bay Area. The Association of Bay Area Governments was organized "for the permanent establishment of a forum for discussion and study of metropolitan area problems of mutual interest and concern . . . and for the development of policy and action recommendations." At present 85 of 92 cities and seven of nine counties in the region are members. Special districts and other units of local government participate in

ABAG as non-voting members.

The San Francisco Bay region is home to many single-purpose agencies, including the Bay Conservation and Development Commission (BCDC), Metropolitan Transportation Commission (MTC), Bay Area Sewage Services Agency (BASSA), Bay Area Air Pollution Control District, and two Regional Coastal Zone Conservation Commissions. In light of its function as the area-wide comprehensive planning agency, ABAG considers close cooperation with these agencies indispensable. ABAG has formed a joint policy committee with MTC to review land-use issues of the Regional Transportation Plan and has entered into a joint powers agreement with other governmental units to form the Bay Delta Resource Recovery Board. Also, under the terms of the Coastal Zone Conservation Act, ABAG is represented on both Regional Commissions within its jurisdiction. Thus, ABAG has attempted to overcome the fragmentation of planning in the Bay Area.

A major problem hampering the operation of such area-wide associations is the absence of an adequately defined role. Though most COGs have stated their function to be that of a comprehensive regional planning organization, there are many divergent views as to how that is to be carried out. Not only do programs vary greatly from one COG to another, but there is uncertainty within individual COGs as to their proper relationship with previously existing governmental units.

The lack of a well-defined purpose is virtually ensured by the statutory basis for COGs. Most of them are based upon the very general provisions of the Joint Exercise of Powers Act, a law intended to serve equally well as the basis for cooperative library arrangements, convention centers, and intercity street maintenance. The Act is essentially a non-statute, leaving the most important considerations to the voluntary negotiated agreement of the parties.

Thus, in a sense, the state has abdicated its responsibility to federal and local governments. The only planning requirements imposed upon COGs are those set forth as conditions to federal grants-in-aid. Since local governments are the draftsmen of the joint powers agreements, and their elected officials the members of the COG governing body, the real constituency of an association of governments is local government and not the residents of the region.

Whether out of a need to satisfy federal requirements or out of a desire to solve problems which can only be approached from a regional perspective, associations of governments will remain a fact of life for the foreseeable future. Moreover, recent court decisions in California and elsewhere have required that local land-use regulations be adopted within the framework of a comprehensive regional scheme. With such forces underlining the importance of COGs, it seems appropriate that the state legislatively recognize their existence.

2. Statutory Regional Planning Agencies

The state has numerous regional and sub-regional entities, usually single-purpose special districts. Examples: the San Francisco Bay Area Air Pollution Control Board, Bay Area Rapid Transit District (BART), Alameda County Transit District (ACT), the Metropolitan Transportation Commission (MTC), the San Francisco Bay Conservation and Development Commission (BCDC), and the Tahoe Regional Planning Agency (TRPA).

Metropolitan Transportation Commission

The MTC was created as a single-purpose planning agency in 1970. It is a "local area planning agency", independent of state government, to provide comprehensive transportation planning for the region comprised of the City and County of San Francisco and the counties of Alameda, Contra Costa, Marin, Napa, San Mateo, Santa Clara, Solano, and Sonoma. MTC was required to develop a regional transportation plan, including state and federal highways, transbay bridges, mass transit systems and interfaces of multi-modal systems. It was to estimate regional transportation priorities according to these needs, to develop a financial program, and to study the relationship of regional harbors and airports to surface transportation.

In addition to planning and finance, the MTC was given powers for assuring compliance with regional policies. It can review and approve applications for federal and state financial assistance by local governments and transportation districts for their compatibility with the regional transportation plan. Its approval is required for: (a) construction of any new transbay bridge; (b) modification of existing bridges for additional lanes of traffic or rapid transit facilities; (c) any new multi-county transit system using a right of way held by an existing system. MTC is to assist public transit systems to ensure adequate feeder service to multi-county systems.

San Francisco Bay Conservation and Development Commission

BCDC is a regional agency formed as a watchdog over development in and around San Francisco Bay.

Its primary responsibilities are preparation and review of the San Francisco Bay Plan, and administration of its permit system. In order to protect the shoreline and bay, BCDC is empowered to issue or deny permits for any project that would fill, extract materials or substantially change a water, land, or structural use within its jurisdiction. The Commission's jurisdiction is the San Francisco Bay, a strip of 100 feet landward along the bayshore, salt ponds, managed wetlands and certain waterways.

BCDC served in part as a model for the Coastal Zone Initiative (Proposition 20), and under the initiative retains its permit authority through an exemption of San Francisco Bay and adjacent lands from the provisions of the Coastal Act. BCDC has also served as a prototype in many other states for regional agencies with land-use regulatory powers.

Tahoe Regional Planning Agency

The Tahoe Regional Planning Agency was created by a California-Nevada bi-state compact, and a majority of its board membership is from local governments. TRPA's planning is tied to its regulatory authority. The bi-state agreement authorizes the Agency to adopt regulations and policies necessary to implement the Tahoe Regional Plan. Each regulation is to establish a minimum standard applicable throughout the basin, but any city or county may adopt a higher standard. Standards must apply to the following: water purity and clarity; subdivision; zoning; tree removal; solid waste disposal from boats;

mobile home parks; house relocation; outdoor advertising; flood plain protection; soil and sedimentation control; air pollution; and watershed protection.

Nevada added to the compact a proviso that ordinances should be restricted to general and regional matters. Specific local ordinances and policies are left to the states, counties, and cities. Also, TRPA ordinances do not apply to any business or recreational establishment individually licensed by state law if (1) it was licensed prior to February 5, 1968; or (2) it was to be built on land appropriately zoned under an adopted master plan by February 5, 1968. This provision essentially removed gambling casinos (which must be individually licensed in Nevada) from the jurisdiction of the Agency.

A final weakness is the Agency's inability to deny approval to public construction projects. Nevada insisted upon the addition of this provision to the compact, probably on the theory that a bi-state agency should not impede projects of state agencies. In California, however, such projects are subject to the approval of the California Tahoe Regional Planning Agency (CTRPA), a governmental instrument of the State of California.

The states, counties and cities in the region, as well as TRPA, have the authority to enforce the regional general plan. The agency is also empowered to police the region to ensure compliance. The Agency may institute court action to compel a local jurisdiction to enforce TRPA ordinances, but there is no provision enabling citizens to sue the Agency or private violators of the ordinances.

C. LOCAL LEVEL PLANNING

Despite the increased planning activity of regional and state level agencies in recent years, substantial control over land use still rests with local government—those institutions traditionally given power to restrict the use of private property. Cities and counties are required by state law to prepare a general plan for their jurisdiction and to implement the plan by exercising their "police power" to promote the general welfare. Although recent state and regional initiatives in planning resulted from inadequacies in land-use control by individual local government, proposals for reform generally retain a sig-

nificant amount of responsibility at the local level.

1. The Local General Plan

At the local level, planning is conceived of as a guide for the future development of the community. A general plan represents the nearest approximation to a consensus on policy objectives.

The traditional approach to land-use planning began with a projection of future economic growth in the local area, based on economic trends and an estimate of future population size. These were then translated into estimates of future land demand for industrial, commercial, residential, and public uses. The land supply was evaluated in terms of a parcel's location or accessibility, size, availability of utilities, and physical characteristics such as slope and soil quality.

This traditional approach to planning resulted in costly pollution, urban sprawl, loss of prime agricultural land and natural amenities. It led directly to the present reevaluation of the local planning process.

Local land-use planning is now evolving on three fronts. First, the basic objectives and assumptions of planning are being redefined. The quality of the natural environment within and around the urban area has assumed importance alongside the traditional concern for the quality of the man-made environment. Land-use planning is increasingly viewed as a means of deciding how much (as well as where) growth should occur.

Second, there has been an increasing search for usable environmental information and land-use data on which to base planning decisions. The art of cost-benefit analysis is being redefined and broadened through its application to the economics of land use.

Third, the emphasis has shifted toward implementation. Too often plans remained on office shelves, unconsulted, while land-use regulations were determined by factors outside the planning process.

Local governments in California have been the leaders on each of these three fronts. To a large extent, innovative land-use programs have been developed by cities and counties. State law requires each city and county to establish a planning agency. At the city level, the agency may be a planning department, planning commission, or the legislative body itself. Counties must have a planning commission. Although the names and functions vary, the following is generally applicable: The planning *department* undertakes studies requested by the city council or board of supervisors, researches proposals for changes in land use and makes recommendations to the planning commission and the local legislative body. A typical planning department staff would include an architect, an urban planner, economics and graphics specialists, and supporting personnel.

A planning *commission* usually exists alongside the planning department. It is composed of citizens appointed by elected officials, and its functions include preparation of a general plan for the area, periodic review of the plan and recommendations to the legislature for implementing ordinances.

State law requires each planning agency to prepare, and each local legislature to adopt, ''a comprehensive, long-term general plan for the physical development of the county or city'' and any lands outside its boundaries which bear relation to its planning. The plan must be prepared so that the local legislature may adopt it piecemeal or in its entirety, and so that it may be adopted for all or part of the area within the jurisdiction.

Each general plan must include nine elements:

Land Use—Proposed general distribution, location, and uses of land for housing, business, industry, open space (including agriculture, natural resources, recreation, and scenic beauty), education, public buildings and grounds, solid and liquid waste disposal facilities and other categories of public and private uses.

Circulation—Location of existing and proposed major roads, transportation routes, terminals, and other local public utilities and facilities.

Housing—Adequate provision for the housing needs of all economic segments of the local community.

Conservation—Conservation, development, and utilization of natural resources including water, forests, soils, rivers, harbors, fisheries, wildlife, minerals, and other natural resources.

Seismic Safety—Seismic hazards, such as susceptibility to surface ruptures, ground shaking, ground failures and effects of seismically induced waves.

Noise—Noise level contours for existing (and projected) major transportation facilities and recommended site and route designations; maximum levels are to be established for each category of land use.

Scenic Highways—Development, establishment and protection of scenic highways under applicable provisions of the Streets and Highways Code.

Safety—Protection from fires and geologic hazards through, for example, evacuation routes, peak water supply requirements, minimum road widths, clearances around structures and geologic hazard mapping.

Open Space—Lands for natural resources, agriculture, recreation, scenic beauty, watershed, or ground water recharge and wildlife habitat.

The open space element is the only element of the general plan backed by sanctions. All local government actions acquiring, disposing, restricting, or regulating open space must be consistent with the open space plan. So must any building permit, subdivision map or open space zoning ordinance.

Many of the shortcomings of local planning can be

traced to the inadequacies of state enabling legislation. The law attempts to prescribe limits of responsibility, but in doing so it includes unnecessary detail and generalities. It attempts to spell out exact steps, but at the same time ignores many procedures. It attempts to set a standard for the quality of resulting plans, but it has fallen short in the absence of a requirement for adequate funding, staff and organization, and lack of incentives or penalities.

The institutions of local planning prescribed in state law were conceived in a simpler time and a rethinking of the entire structure is in order. The current arrangement has grown up under hesitant, piecemeal guidance from the state. The narrow view of local land-use decisions has been partly caused by decentralized decision-making. The task is divided among professional planners, planning commissions, and local politicians. No state standards are prescribed for commission membership. Even though the position is part-time, commission duties require more time than lower income level persons would be able to deduct from their regular job. Because of the limited time available, commissioners must rely heavily upon the professional planning staffs.

The inferior quality of many plans has long been of concern to the planning profession and, recently, to the Legislature. Requiring an increasing number of planning elements was not as successful as it might have been. Smaller communities are often overburdened by these requirements.

On the other hand, progress at the local level has at times outdistanced the legislative concept of general planning. For example, some local jurisdictions now prepare "community plans" and "private development plans", but these innovations are nowhere reflected in state law. Perhaps the most serious omission affecting general plans is the absence of any method for enforcement of the state planning requirements. Deadlines for general plan elements have been adopted, but local governments which do not comply suffer no penalities or sanctions. No general provisions for citizen enforcement exist in the planning law.

Because general plans themselves have no direct legal effect, there is often a gap between a plan and its implementation. Until recently, and the adoption of the consistency requirement, cities were able to pass zoning ordinances without any reference to the long range objectives of the general plan. A 1973 survey of local planning departments in California found that 48 percent of the counties and 56 percent of the cities had zoning ordinances inconsistent with their general plan.

Recognizing this discrepancy, the Legislature recently required that zoning be made consistent with the general plan. However, the new requirement has created uncertainty among local officials and it is not clear that planning and its implementation will be more closely related than before.

2. Implementation of the General Plan

Adoption of a general plan by cities and counties has no direct impact on land use. Because the plan itself has no legal effect, it is commonly implemented by a wide variety of land-use controls. When local planning was in its infancy, zoning ordinances and other regulations constituted a de facto "plan" because such controls were the only constraints on development. As planning has become more sophisticated, new types of controls have been devised.

Zoning

The tool most frequently employed to regulate the use of privately owned land is zoning. The most traditional type of zoning is *use zoning*. Cities and counties may regulate the use of land and buildings by restricting areas for industrial, business, residential, agricultural, and other purposes.

Early zoning ordinances were based upon a scale of intensity, with single-family residential the least intense use and heavy industrial use the most intense. These projections of distinct bands of residential, commercial, and industrial uses for every community soon proved impractical. Modern zoning is a more flexible and ad hoc device:

Cluster zoning provides for a fixed ratio of housing units to acreage and requires that the units be "clustered," or built close together. A landowner who plans to subdivide his parcel would be permitted to build his quota of houses on only a small portion of the land, leaving the rest for open space.

Floating zoning is a more flexible approach. A "floating district" is described in the zoning ordinance, but the district is not located on the zoning map until the need arises. The ordinance simply describes what can be done in the floating district, such as building apartment houses, and lists the circumstances under which the city council will consider zoning property for this use.

Planned unit development zoning is a type of floating

zone which applies to parcels of land which are to be developed as a "single entity", according to a comprehensive plan. The zoning unit generally contains a residential housing cluster of prescribed density and the appropriate commercial and institutional facilities to serve the residents.

Conditional, or contract zoning is the most flexible zoning device and enables a city or county to bargain with developers for certain concessions. A city, for example, may agree to rezone land in a residential district for a hospital, but require the developer to surround the hospital with trees and take steps to blend it into the neighborhood.

Interim zoning imposes a moratorium on building, clearing trees or tearing down historical landmarks while the city considers whether to purchase the area or rezone it.

Subdivision Regulation

Although zoning is the most common tool used by local government to implement the general plan, the "police power" also enables cities and counties to control development through subdivision regulations.

The conversion of large amounts of open space land to suburban development through subdivision can have a great impact on the ability of the local government to enforce its general plan. Developers must file maps of their proposed subdivision with the local government, which has authority to give approval, disapproval, or conditional approval.

Recognizing the need to control subdivisions, state law now requires "consistency" between any proposed subdivision and all applicable general and specific plans. If the city council or board of supervisors finds the proposed subdivision inconsistent, then the subdivision map may not be approved.

The power to regulate subdivision is exercised by requiring the dedication of land in return for approving the tentative map, or by withholding approval of the map altogether. Cities and counties may attach many conditions to approval, and may exact from the developer land or fees which are used toward costs of supporting services otherwise imposed on the community as a whole.

Urban Renewal

The redevelopment of an urban area can promote or frustrate implementation of the local general plan. Urban renewal involves all levels of government being funded by the federal government, controlled by the state enabling legislation, and administered at the local level. It utilizes planning, zoning, subdivision regulation, building codes and many other land-use controls to bring the redevelopment project to completion.

Federal incentives for the elimination of slums and blighted areas take the form of grants to local renewal agencies. Many conditions are attached to these funds: the project must be in accord with an urban renewal plan which must in turn conform to the general plan of the community. This plan must indicate proposed land acquisition, historic preservation, rehabilitation and demolition sites. Local government must adopt a workable program for community improvements as approved by the Department of Housing and Urban Development.

To enable local governments to participate in the federal urban renewal program, the state Legislature has provided for the creation of a redevelopment agency for each community. The jurisdiction of a county agency is the unincorporated area of the county, and a city agency operates within the city limits.

The local agency may acquire land by purchase, lease, or eminent domain; relocate displaced persons; make site preparations; build some types of structures; and sell acquired land.

Local government supervises the renewal agency's activities, and the agency must also conduct a biennial public hearing on the plan and its implementation.

Housing Authority

A housing authority is a separate non-profit corporate body apart from the city or county in which it operates. Its general powers include the construction, acquisition and operation of "housing projects," which are defined as an undertaking financed in whole or in part by the federal or state government to provide sanitary and safe dwellings in urban or rural areas. In the exercise of its powers, a housing authority is subject to all planning, zoning and building ordinances.

The creation of housing agencies is a matter of local determination since the state legislation merely enables cities and counties to undertake housing programs. Two or more cities and counties in any combination may agree to form an area housing council, which then develops a plan. Local governments may adopt this as the housing element of its general plan, in which case it must conform to the CIR guidelines. Upon such adoption, the city is entitled to half its proportionate share of the council's surcharge on local building permits, and these funds may be used only to implement the housing element of the general plan. The commissioners of an area housing council are the planning director of each member jurisdiction, the executive director of the housing authority of each jurisdiction and two commissioners appointed by the local legislatures "who shall be representative of the housing and construction industry."

Growth Management

Subdivision regulation, many forms of zoning, and urban renewal programs can all be important tools by which to implement the general plan. However, some local governments have found that, in addition to determining the eventual shape of development, they must also guide its timing and location.

One effect of uncontrollable growth is an overburdening of water, sewage, and other public services. In response to such problems, some communities have placed a moratorium on further development until planning is completed, regulations are adopted, and public facilities are expanded. For example, a city ordinance could simply declare that no more building permits for residential construction will be issued until certain standards for the provision of public services are met. In one Northern California city, "satisfactory solutions" to the problem of inadequate facilities were identified as no double sessions in the schools or no overcrowded classrooms as determined by the California Education Code, sewage treatment facilities in compliance with the standards of the Regional Water Quality Control Board and no rationing of drinking water.

Programs to guide the timing and sequence of development are sometimes referred to as "phased zoning." One form of "phased zoning" does not in fact rezone any property. Rather, land already designated for residential use in the future can not be subdivided for development until the landowner obtains a special permit from the city council. This permit is granted only if the landowner can show the availability of adequate public services such as sewers, drainage, park sites, and roads. Thus, development in the restricted area would be "phased" as the city is willing and able to extend public services.

A similar system incorporates as criteria many aspects of development beyond the availability of public services: provision of open space by the developer, low and moderate income housing, and architectural design quality. Under this scheme, the city can encourage the particular type of development it desires.

Property Taxation

California law enables city and county governments to give tax advantages to landowners who devote their property to open space and agricultural uses. Until 1966, the California Constitution required property tax assessors to value land at its "highest and best use." The result was that a farmer living near a city paid taxes on the speculative value of his land as a subdivision rather than on its present value for agricultural use. The dynamics of the market increased the value of land near urban centers, forcing owners to sell or develop their property.

A state constitutional amendment in 1966 authorized assessment of open space and agricultural lands at their actual rather than speculative use if the land was subject to an "enforceable restriction." Such restrictions limit the use of the land to recreation, enjoyment of scenic beauty, use of natural resources, or production of food or fiber.

The most commonly used form of tax incentive is the California Land Conservation Act (1965) popularly known as the Williamson Act. This Act enables cities and counties to form "agricultural preserves" and to enter into contract with owners of land. Once land is under the Williamson Act, it qualifies for a special valuation for property tax purposes, based on actual use rather than "highest and best use".

Environmental Impact Assessment

The California Environmental Quality Act of 1970 requires that "all agencies of the state government which regulate activities of private individuals, corporations, and public agencies . . . shall regulate such activities so that major consideration is given to preventing environmental damage." To carry this out, an environmental impact report must be prepared prior to approval or disapproval of any activity having a significant environmental effect. EIR's are prepared for "projects" on an individual basis. The governmental units which are required to prepare them include any state agency, board or commission, any county, city, regional agency or "other political subdivision." Projects subject to EIR's are also broadly defined to encompass activities directly undertaken by the agency, activities funded wholly or partly by governmental agencies, and the issuance of permits, certificates or "other entitlement."

An environmental impact report is required when three conditions are met. First, the project must be one which will have a "significant effect" on the "environment." Environment is described as only those physical conditions, not social or economic factors, within the area which will be affected by a proposed project.

Second, the project must be discretionary, and not a ministerial or an emergency activity. Ministerial projects are routine activities where the agency has no power to approve or disapprove. Discretionary projects include the inactment and amendment of zoning ordinances, issuance of zoning variances, issuance of conditional use permits and approval of tentative subdivision maps.

Third, the project must not be "categorically exempt." Categorically exempt activities include replacement or reconstruction, new construction of small structures and minor alterations to land.

Local Agency Formation Commission

There is an obvious relationship between land-use patterns and governmental services. Policies which create or alter local public service have important applications for land-use planning.

The rapid population increase in California following World War II generated increasing demands for governmental services. Cities frequently competed to expand their territory by annexing nearby, unincorporated areas—an activity which resulted in contrived and illogical municipal boundaries and shapes. Local Agency Formation Commissions were created by the state to deal with this organizational problem.

LAFCO's have authority over the growth of cities and the multiplication of special districts. Special districts are defined as instruments of the state for the local performance of governmental functions within limited boundaries. This includes county service areas, but not special assessment and improvement districts, or school districts.

A LAFCO operates at the county level, and is to discourage urban sprawl and to insure the orderly formation and development of cities and special districts. LAFCOs are required to initiate studies of existing cities and special districts so as to determine their maximum service areas and capabilities.

In addition, each LAFCO is to determine the "sphere of influence"—or the probable ultimate boundary and service area—of each city and special district within its jurisdiction. No power is given to a LAFCO to initiate changes, however; it must wait for proposals to be submitted.

Airport Land-Use Commissions

Counties with a population of less than four million persons may create an Airport Land-Use Commission to study and recommend uses and restrictions of land surrounding airports. (Counties with a population of more than four million persons are to designate the County Planning Commission as the responsible agency.)

Airport Land-Use Commissions are authorized to study and make recommendations concerning (a) the need for height restrictions on buildings near airports; (b) land uses surrounding airports. The commissions may also formulate comprehensive land-use plans for areas surrounding public airports to provide for the orderly growth of each public airport and surrounding area and to safeguard the general welfare of the inhabitants within the vicinity of the airport.

However, the authority of the Airport Land-Use Commissions is limited. Their findings are not binding, but are advisory only to the involved jurisdictions. They will never achieve the purpose for which they are created unless decision-making and regulatory powers are provided to accompany their planning functions.

Conclusions

The proliferation of single purpose agencies, special districts, and ad hoc commissions has been an obstacle to the solution to the state's real environmental quality and growth distribution problems. This fragmentation has avoided the fundamental questions about California's future.

Given the absence of an explicit and effective state planning process and policy, it was inevitable that a substantial land-use vacuum would develop. It was also inevitable that de facto substitutes would fill that vacuum with the "backdoor" land-use planning of single purpose agencies.

The question now is not whether the state should initiate land-use policy planning—for indeed, in bits and pieces, we have already begun—but when and how the existing plans can be integrated so that they serve clear state land-use policies rather than the needs of various departments, programs, and special interest groups.

California's planning law, processes and institutions stand in desperate need of serious revision.

Chapter Two

ISSUES AND FINDINGS

In this chapter we present the results of our consideration of eight key issues involved in land-use planning, together with our findings. These findings, which represent the consensus of members of the California Land-Use Task Force, are offered as guidelines for specific areas of policy formation.

Although this material is arranged under eight separate headings, it must be emphasized that each of the subjects connects to all the others: the rehabilitation of our cities and the protection of our agricultural lands are compatible goals and are related to other issues such as energy, resources, transportation, housing, compensation, and taxation. In some cases, specific needs can be detached and dealt with separately, but it has become increasingly necessary to look at the entire picture of California land use and to understand that activities in one policy area invariably have consequences in another.

1. CITIES

The post World War II years of California's housing boom were a period of growth and prosperity and, at the same time, a period of deterioration and decline. The growth was in the suburbs. The deterioration was primarily in the old urban areas of California—areas that had once been vital and attractive centers of residences, business and cultural activity.

This has been a complex and rapid change, and the reasons for it are still not clearly understood. Following are some of the factors which are believed to have contributed:

Forces Contributing to the Development of New Urban Areas

- Rising income and population growth, resulting in a demand for millions of new housing units.
- Development of the freeway system which made it possible for urban workers to live in the new and more spacious suburban areas.
- The desire of small and middle-sized cities to grow, prompting them to acquire rural land by incorporation and to encourage development of new business and residential properties.
- The greater simplicity and—from the viewpoint of developers and builders—substantially smaller cost in acquiring land, providing necessary services, and building commercial and residential structures by economic mass production techniques on vacant rural lands rather than in cities.
- New styles of business and factory operation which made it preferable for businesses to design new structures to fit their needs and build them on open land, rather than adapt to their new needs old structures designed for an earlier era.

Forces Contributing to the Decline of Old Urban Areas

- The diminished support for providing convenient public transportation systems, accompanied by the increased popularity of the personal automobile.
- Social change which brought conflict to public schools in areas where populations and education styles were not homogeneous, and where no satisfactory accomodation to diversity could be made.
- Changes in perception of the seat of power and responsibility for city wellbeing, from city government toward federal government.
- The decision by large numbers of educated, forceful, and ambitious people that old cities and downtowns were not a place to live, with a result that the dynamism of these people as a resource to maintain the vitality of cities was lost.
- Taxation policies and building codes which discouraged retention, maintenance, or improvement of older properties.
- Construction of freeways through inner city areas.

Return deteriorating and underused urban areas to high productive use.
(Finding 1, page 37.)

33

Consequences of the Decline

The result for the older cities has been undesirable, if not disastrous. Large areas of old city land are vacant or underutilized. Employment possibilities have diminished. There are extensive areas of concentration of unemployed, underemployed, underprivileged minorities, and ill-cared for aged. In these areas, parks and recreation facilities are run down or non-existent. Houses are in disrepair. Persons displaced by urban renewal programs are unable to find new housing. Retired persons are forced to give up their homes because of rising taxes. Street crime and inadequate public transportation stifle the possibility of recreation and ability to move around. Retail businesses decline or disappear. The city too often, in sum, fails to offer employment, places to shop, pleasant places to live, recreation, beauty, sound education and opportunity to participate freely and confidently in an exhilarating city life.

This has been universally perceived as undesirable and regrettable. Many attempts, with an expenditure of billions of dollars, have been made to cure the situation. Most agree that less than full success has attended these attempts, though no one knows what condition the cities would be in if the attempts had not been made. Federally financed urban renewal programs sometimes successfully stemmed a city's decline, but often simultaneously created new problems by eliminating scarce housing and by creating large areas which stood empty of residences or businesses for years.

Moreover, the citizens of a city often perceived a program as an inappropriate and unwanted plan imposed upon them. People lost the sense of belonging to communities. They felt powerless to shape the future of their own areas—often with reason, for political boundaries were so drawn that poor and minority districts had no real representation on local governing boards.

The lack of more than minimal success created a climate where the plight of old cities had come to be tolerated as inevitable and incapable of solution.

State and City Strategies

This acceptance of inevitability must and probably has come to a halt. Underuse and misuse of city land is no longer merely regrettable; it is intolerable. Better use should be made of existing urbanized areas for new businesses and residences, for reasons which include the following:

- Cities cannot continue to turn to agricultural land to meet their housing needs. There must be an increasing inward focus. Older city land must be used if we are to provide more housing and employment opportunities nearby.
- Energy must be conserved. City residences and businesses are more energy efficient, particularly with respect to transportation.
- Political pressure requires that aesthetically pleasing open space adjacent to urban areas be preserved.
- Neither the social waste of the present underemployed and ill-housed inner-city residents, nor the deterioration of cities as cultural centers for all the people, can be tolerated by responsible citizens.

The revitalization of deteriorating urban areas is a keystone to a successful state land-use plan. The state must take the lead to revitalize our cities in three ways. First, it should undertake a review of laws and policies to determine where they act as impediments to city revitalization and maintenance, and how they should be revised. Examples include building codes, zoning, assessment practices and the property tax structure. Where revision is indicated, appropriate legislation should be enacted.

Second, the state should act as advisor to cities in their formulation of plans for revitalization as well as their general plans. Cities should have primary responsibility for planning and carrying out local programs, and they must involve their citizens in

35

Find methods for the state, the cities, and the private financial sector to cooperate in the restoration process.

(Finding 3, page 37.)

the planning, decision-making, and implementation of their programs. Cities usually lack, however, deep and broad expertise, and are overwhelmed by the magnitude of the problems which face them. The state, through its Department of Housing and Community Development, should provide high quality professional, technical, and planning assistance, as well as procedures for timely communication of relevant and available federal financial and planning aids.

Third, the state should examine in partnership with cities and the private financial sector what appropriate role it should play in financing the restoration and maintenance process. State and cities should solicit the participation of the private financial community so as to get the maximum benefit of the experience and resources of private enterprise. Financing of local programs will be considerably assisted by money made available to communities under the Federal Housing and Community Development Act of 1974. The state for its part should consider what methods of financial support it should provide which will make possible sound programs at reasonable cost to cities and the state as a whole. Possible support methods include subsidies, provision of high risk revolving loan funds, loan guarantees, and bond financing.

FINDINGS/CITIES

1. It is urgent that deteriorating and underused urban areas be revitalized and returned to high productive use. Such productive use includes housing for the whole income spectrum, commerce and industry, public services, recreational and cultural facilities.

2. The state should act as advisor to local units of government in formulating their revitalization plans. Assistance should include high quality professional, technical, and planning expertise, as well as timely communication of relevant and available federal financial and planning aids.

3. The state should carefully examine, in cooperation with cities and the private financial sector, methods by which city and state action can encourage the restoration process. Possible methods are subsidies, provision of high risk revolving loan funds, loan guarantees, and issuance of bonds.

4. The flexibility and careful attention which private financing groups can bring to bear on a problem should be utilized. Programs should therefore be structured to encourage strong participation by private financing.

5. The financial needs of each city are different, but common elements are:

- financial advice
- suitably structured loans
- bond issues

These are needed for:

- rehabilitation of residences and commercial buildings;
- purchase of older homes;
- construction of new housing for low/moderate-income and senior citizen residents;
- physical improvement of downtown areas;
- business loans;
- acquisition of amenities such as parks, open space, and recreation areas;
- financing of transportation systems, infrastructure and other community services.

6. Where local or state ordinances, statutes, regulations or required procedures impede revitalization and restoration, they should be re-examined and changed. Examples include building codes, zoning assessment practices, and tax laws. In particular, the property tax structure should be reviewed in order to eliminate tax pressure against property maintenance and improvement.

7. Cities should find or require adequate replacement housing for people displaced by revitalization programs.

8. As recommended elsewhere in this report, new residential and business growth should take place within existing urban boundaries and in areas designated for new urbanization.

9. Citizens must be involved in the planning, decision-making and implementation of urban revitalization programs.

10. Employment opportunities should be directed to inner city areas where under-employed groups live.

2. HOUSING

Although birth rates are down, California's population is still growing and will continue to do so. And the demand for housing will grow faster than the population itself. Housing is a measure of the number of households, and this decade will see a household boom as the people born since World War II seek their own places to live. Between 1974 and 1978, a total of 952,000 new housing units will have to be built in California. And at least another million units should be restored or torn down and replaced to house the very large number of people who live in rundown, substandard, or overcrowded units.

Such are the needs. It is easy to say that they must be met. But we must admit at the start that they cannot possibly be met with present tools.

The housing industry in California is in trouble. Costs have risen enormously. Housing prices have been going up much faster than the consumer price index. The poor, not surprisingly, are being hit hardest: but the ''poor'', when it comes to buying new housing, may soon be half the population. The price of the least expensive housing has been rising fastest of all, and it appears that housing on the free market will become almost a luxury item.

According to the state, California needs 600,000 new housing units with rent or payments under $60 a month. This is a need which the housing market of the 1970's simply cannot meet, given its present situation. Mobile homes have been the answer for many people. In 1973, one in every five single-family housing units built in the state was a mobile home. But even this housing is rapidly pricing itself out of reach: the average cost of a mobile home pad is up in two years from $3,200 to over $5,000 and still rising. In several areas, such as the Hemet-Sun City area, hundreds of mobile home pads go unoccupied.

Another possible answer is public or subsidized housing. But the programs of the federal government have not yet made much of a difference. Suspension of the 236 (low income rental) program and the unsuccessful 235 (low income housing) program of the 1968 Housing and Urban Development Act have left a void in subsidized housing.

There are about 60,000 units of public housing in the state—enough to absorb about three percent of the households which meet the income requirements. There is obviously a tremendous gap. The new Section 8, authorized by the Housing Act of 1974, even if fully implemented, cannot serve it completely. Private development must be stimulated and given direction.

The housing problem has existed for decades. Now in our current economic climate, the problem has become a crisis.

In the past, the need for low-income housing has often been used as an argument for unrestricted development, but decades of development have not solved the housing problems of the poor.

Meanwhile, other considerations such as open space have been pushed aside. We can now see that we must not only provide housing but at the same time protect open space and ensure the proper use of land.

Where and How

''How much'' is only one of the questions to be asked about housing. We must also look at the ''where'' and ''how'' of residential growth, and ask: can we afford to accommodate the new generation of families in the same manner as the last? Will the

Provide people of all incomes with adequate housing at prices they can afford.
(Finding 1, page 44.)

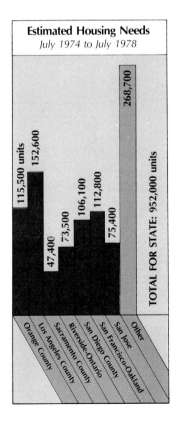

Estimated Housing Needs
July 1974 to July 1978

115,500 units — Orange County
152,600 — Los Angeles County
47,400 — Sacramento County
73,500 — Riverside-Ontario
106,100 — San Diego County
112,800 — San Francisco-Oakland
75,400 — San Jose
268,700 — Other
TOTAL FOR STATE: 952,000 units

Locate new residential growth within already urbanized areas, and within other areas specifically designated to receive growth.

(Finding 6, page 44.)

economy and energy/resource shortages even permit us to do so?

Most of the housing built in the last decade was on the urban fringe. Nationwide, the suburbs took 70 percent of the U.S. population growth. In California, because of low-density building, the total land area covered by housing increased even faster than the suburban population.

This thin-spread urban fabric has often covered lands which might better have been preserved for crop production, for recreation, or simply for their natural beauty. The landscape of single-family detached houses has become a symbol of California.

This pattern of development occurred for several basic reasons, foremost of which was the preference for inexpensive land which would easily lend itself to development. Consumers were attracted to the suburban lifestyle. However, we can now see that this lifestyle has serious disadvantages. Most workers must travel many miles to their jobs, usually by car. Everyone pays for this in increased air pollution and energy consumption. Irregular and rapid development has left many suburban areas without complete urban facilities and services—and the cost of services, because of the long distances, is high.

Developers, drawn to more inexpensive land in the suburbs, have turned away from the older developed areas: commercial centers in the suburbs, designed for shoppers in cars, draw business from the older central districts. Indirectly, new development has contributed to the decay of older urban areas.

Why did development take this form? Because land prices were low. Because the demand for single-family houses, far from the problems of the city, was unquestionably strong. Because new freeways and cheap gasoline permitted the 100-mile commute. And because few at the time saw cause to worry much about the cost to both the city and the land.

Now of course many of these things are no longer true. We are seeing a great reversal, caused by both political and economic changes. Today, in many parts of California, single-family housing is strictly a luxury item. The mass market is confined to existing housing or new higher density housing. As we move into a period of shortages, the development style of the 1960's will become more and more impractical.

But we cannot assume that high densities, clustering, and other innovations will automatically produce the kind of urban landscape we want. In some suburban areas, where the new methods are widely used, one sees both advantages and problems. Housing covers less ground; yet it continues to scatter itself over wide landscapes, in cluster and strip developments separated by random parcels of open space (often land too steep to be built on). This arrangement avoids some, but not all, of the problems of the sixties-style suburban sprawl. With higher densities, it is important that amenities not be thrown away: that usable open space be near at hand, that privacy and silence be assured, that the natural environment not be simply eliminated where people live.

The Development Approval Process

Except in some special cases, it is still most often the city or county government that decides where new housing development occurs and what it looks like.

Until recently, City Councils and Boards of Supervisors were mainly uncritical of development proposals. Local general plans were not taken seriously. In many

Locate housing and employment close together.

(Finding 10, page 45.)

40

places, it was policy to welcome growth, providing facilities for it at general public expense.

That was the old climate. Today, even the developer understands that the seventies will be different. Instead of seeking growth or simply making room for it, officials talk of guiding it, limiting it, moderating it, controlling it, or even stopping it.

So the developer's job is much more difficult. Builders are confronted with requirements for environmental impact reports and open space dedications. They are faced with the delays caused by permit procedures before such bodies as the Bay Conservation and Development Commission, TRPA, the Coastal Commissions, and even, on occasion, the Army Corps of Engineers. Whenever there is controversy (and today with a large project there always is) there will be long delay. With each delay the price to be asked for the completed housing goes up.

It is hard to question the need for a closer scrutiny of planned development. Yet not even the skeptics defend the approval system as it stands, the long gauntlet to be run by any plan. The process is complex. It is arbitrary. Its procedures change continually. It may take an interested citizen of any persuasion months to understand how to make his opinions felt.

The Environmental Impact Report

The environmental impact report on private development—required by the California Environmental Quality Act of 1970—is one attempt to do the job better. It is obviously of value to identify alternatives to a proposed project and weigh the environmental consequences of each. However, the EIR has tended to be a justification of a decision already made rather than an exploration of possible choices. Those who write EIRs must struggle with key issues that really should be dealt with in the general plan level EIRs, rather than project by project.

Growth Controls

Recently the regulation of development by local government has taken a new direction. Governments now seek to control, not only the details of development, but also the rates and amount of growth. Some localities seek to put ceilings on their popula-

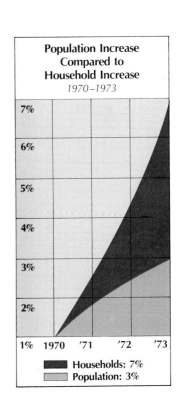

Population Increase Compared to Household Increase
1970–1973

7%
6%
5%
4%
3%
2%
1% 1970 '71 '72 '73

■ Households: 7%
■ Population: 3%

tions. Projects are being examined with a canny eye to profit and loss: will the new construction require services worth more than it yields in taxes? And in some areas, voters are stopping or slowing development by turning down the expansion of water or sewage facilities.

Unfortunately, in some cases growth controls have been motivated by selfish interests. Yet in many places the argument for limits to growth is compelling. The question is not whether such measures make sense, but whether local governments should be the ones to have this responsibility. After all, if growth is turned aside from one place, it increases the pressure somewhere else. These decisions go far beyond the boundaries of one jurisdiction. Like the purely local growth-promoting policies of the past, purely local growth-limiting policies are not satisfactory. Allocation of housing must be done areawide, and be consistent with state land-use policies.

This is not a totally new concept. There are already state and regional agencies that may step in to limit growth from a wider perspective. Water pollution control agencies often impose moratoria when sewage treatment is inadequate, and air pollution boards will soon have to do the same for much larger areas to meet the requirements of the Clean Air Act of 1970.

Urban Limit Lines

Another alternative is an "urban limit" to stop the horizontal expansion of cities at a definite line.

After twenty years of spreading low-density development, the governments of the Sacramento area began to take a new look at their general plans. Total population figures from all local plans showed three times the population there was any reason to expect. Using a lower population figure, regional planners proposed that local governments confine development to: developed land; land surrounded or outflanked by development; or land near existing or committed service hookups.

As a result, the city of Sacramento has cut by 40 percent the amount of land zoned for development within its limits.

Housing and Planning

Today, builders see government presenting a variety of building codes; creating layers of land-use regulation; condemning older homes as inadequate, undesirable

Streamline decision-making throughout government to clarify the development process.

(Finding 12, page 45.)

42

or unsafe; and questioning traditional cost-benefit relationships in new construction. Processing time for government programs has often been prohibitively expensive.

The state must assume a strong leadership role to deal with the housing crisis. Where responsibility is delegated to other levels of government, it should be supported by effective legal authority and adequate funds. State and regional plans should develop criteria for selecting growth and no-growth areas and should clearly identify areas designated for residential growth. This process will have to consider the natural, social and economic conditions in each area, and will have to take into account the need for a mix of ages, races, and income levels in housing developments.

In addition, the private sector must be given incentives to rehabilitate and develop the inner cities. Preservation of farmlands will merely put pressure on other lands unless a system is provided to simplify any phase planned development. A planning mechanism for environmentally sound land-use is the only way the dual goals of adequate housing and protection of agricultural lands can be achieved.

New Towns and Development Areas

Housing and development cannot, however, occur entirely within existing cities. New towns, planned from the ground up, might also contribute to the solution of housing problems. State land-use planning will have to designate suitable areas and provide support programs tor infrastructure and economic base development.

FINDINGS/HOUSING

1. People of all incomes should have adequate housing at prices they can afford. Strong state policies and programs should work toward this goal.

2. Where the state gives responsibility for carrying out these policies to other levels of government, it must also provide legal authority and adequate funds.

3. There should be a process for allocating low and moderate income housing on an area-wide basis, in combination with employment, education, and other opportunities.

4. Government should provide incentives to help the private sector meet the largest possible proportion of housing needs, consistent with state land-use policies. State and federal subsidies will be necessary to provide adequate low-income housing.

5. The state should establish policies on the location of residential growth, designate specific urban and agricultural growth centers, and establish "urban limit" lines around existing urban centers. The plans and actions of all levels of government should be consistent with these policies.

6. New residential growth should occur within already urbanized areas, and within other areas specifically designated to receive growth. The State Land Use Plan should identify those areas of the state best suited to permanent urban use and designate them as "urban growth areas." Both existing and potentially suitable areas should be evaluated, taking into consideration social, economic and environmental criteria including but not limited to:

- public safety: avoid areas prone to flood, fire, landslide, and extreme earthquake hazard
- the carrying capacities of land, water, air
- the ability to provide urban infrastructure

- the fiscal condition of local governments
- the need to maintain and improve the existing housing stock
- ability to achieve a definite and compatible future interface with designated agricultural or open space areas
- land configuration
- ability to provide a range of housing types and price ranges serving a diverse cross-section of lifestyle choices and economic means.

7. The carrying capacity of some areas already has been exceeded. The designation of new residential growth must take this into account and help to alleviate the problem if possible, not aggravate it.

8. Though higher densities in housing are to be expected, amenities should not be sacrificed. In developed areas—as well as in areas designated for new growth—useful and accessible open space must be provided, and other elements of a liveable environment must be preserved.

9. Revitalization of housing and business development within older urban areas cannot occur without supporting services and code modifications of local government.

10. Housing and employment should be close together.

11. The process of acting upon proposed developments at the local level should be simplified and shortened, while providing for necessary environmental and planning analysis.

12. The state should make every effort to streamline decision-making throughout government to clarify the development process.

13. Land-use planning for the state must be seen as a mechanism to assist in providing needed housing for all citizens.

14. A mix of ages, races, and income should be encouraged in housing development.

3. AGRICULTURE

The importance of our farm and forest lands—to the state, the nation, and the world—is unquestionable. Yet we are removing them from agricultural use at a significant rate.

California originally had approximately 8,700,000 acres of land of highest quality soil.[1] Today there are about 7,000,000 acres left; and of these approximately 500,000 acres are zoned for urban development within the next decade.[2]

California's agriculture is one of the most diversified in the world, with no one crop dominating the state's farm economy. This is illustrated by the fact that most crops individually count for less than two percent of the state's total gross farm income. California leads the nation by a wide margin in the production of fruits and vegetables and maintains about 8,000,000 acres under irrigation, largely for the production of specialty crops.

With these attributes, California supplies not only 25 percent of the entire amount of table foods consumed in the United States and 40 percent of the fresh vegetables and fruits, but also accounts for a significant 10 percent of the United States' agricultural exports.[3] In a time of rising prices and world-wide food shortages, the demand for California's agricultural products will increase. According to a recent University of California study, "California will play a significant role among the developed nations of the world in confronting . . . the food problems of the future."[4]

California's agricultural industry generated about $5 billion worth of products in 1972. This increased to $7.2 billion in 1973 and it is anticipated that the increased production of agricultural products in California, coupled with increasing prices, will boost the value of California agricultural production to $9 billion in 1985 and $18 billion by the year 2000.[5] This is more than twice the farm income of any other state. We cut more timber than any other state except Oregon. Together farming, ranching, and logging contribute more to the gross state product than any other industry.

Irrigation is the key to California's great agricultural wealth, even though only a small fraction of the total land area is irrigated. Most of the state's productive farm land receives only 15 inches or less of rainfall a year. Expansion of irrigated lands has risen from a mere 60,000 acres in 1870 to 8,600,000 acres in 1970 and the total is expected to reach 9,100,000 acres by 1980.[6]

The state's agricultural economy and overall crop yield have increased substantially during the post-war period of urbanization, which displaced vast acreages of productive agricultural soils. There was a net loss in agricultural lands due to this urbanization prior to the 1960s; however, in the early 1960s the trend reversed itself, and according to the 1974 Prime Agricultural Lands Report of The Office of Planning and Research, "California gains approximately 56,000 acres of irrigated agricultural land per year net. This figure is an annual average net gain taken over a 12 year period between 1960-1972." The gain, of course, is in irrigated acreage, not prime agricultural land.

The OPR report states that California currently has 12,500,000 acres of "prime" agricultural lands,[7] plus 7,800,000 acres of "potential prime"[8] for a total agricultural land resource of 20,300,000 acres. Of this amount, 620,000 acres of "prime" lands and 463,000 acres of "potential prime" lands lie within an estimated "1985 urban development zone." The report also notes that "during the past two decades Califor-

Provide for the preservation of agricultural lands and their management under principles of sustained yield.

(Finding 1, page 53.)

47

Revise taxation and assessment practices so that they support the preservation of prime agricultural lands.

(Finding 6, page 53.)

nia has lost approximately 15-20,000 acres of 'highly productive agricultural land' per year to urban uses."

Losses of prime agricultural land have traditionally been mitigated by making the desert bloom through transfers of water from one region to another, utilization of cheap energy for intensive forms of agriculture and other technological advances. These losses have come at too high a price at all levels of our society in the form of economic, social, and environmental problems.

The time has come to take effective steps to preserve agricultural lands. We must be certain that the inputs of energy and the net returns from food produced provide the people of the state and the world at large the finest form of nutrition at the most reasonable cost. To achieve this goal will require intensive study and review of current practices where the mix of resources—land, water, energy, capital, technology, and manpower—are coordinated to produce our basic needs of nutrition through quality food.

The productivity of our agricultural lands is not the only reason for valuing them. They frame and separate the great urban areas and make the landscape more attractive. Properly managed, they help keep the air clean and recharge the ground with fresh water. Ideally the wise preservation of agricultural land compliments urban growth—shaping urban centers, preventing urban sprawl and concentrating urban services such as transportation, with savings in energy and resources.

Despite its obvious and many-sided value, the land has not been preserved. Some 1,700,000 acres of cropland are now cities and suburbs, and urbanization continues. How does this happen?

First of all, the market places a higher value on the land for development than for farming. Second, the land on the urban fringe tends to be cheaper than land within the city—which encourages its use in place of full utilization of urban space. Third, the property tax system which values land at its "highest and best use" increases the tax burden on farmers and makes agriculture unprofitable. Even before development takes place, adjacent development, high land prices, high taxes, and other pressures induce farmers to sell out.

Another kind of urban impact upon agriculture is pollution: yields go down as the smog layer thickens. In 1969 the state estimated a loss of $44.5 million due to air pollution, much of it to citrus crops in the South Coast Air Basin.[9]

Urbanization is not the only problem. There are ways of damaging agricultural land without paving it. According to the Soil Conservation Service, 60,000 acre-feet of soil a year are lost as a result of logging, construction work, and farming and flood control practices. Our 10,000,000 acres of rangeland are not being properly managed, nor are our forests.

One of the most remarkable things about California agriculture is the fact that crop yields overall have not decreased during the period of massive urbanization. Some good soils not previously farmed were brought under irrigation. Some previously mediocre soils were irrigated and fertilized into high yields. But this replacement agriculture does not come cheap.

The capital cost of replacing old lands with new is high. There is increasing controversy about costs of energy-intensive agriculture dependent upon irrigation and chemical fertilizers.

Present Controls

The state government lacks effective powers to preserve agricultural land. City and county governments have generally encouraged suburban growth. The effort of other agencies with some interest—coastal commissions, pollution control agencies, councils of government—are fragmented. The strongest action has been taken by certain counties—such as Marin, Napa, Sacramento, and Ventura—which have created agricultural zones allowing one dwelling to each 20, 40, 60, and 80 acres.

The state has tried to protect agriculture by the indirect method of offering tax incentives to owners of agriculture land. The Williamson Act (California Land Conservation Act of 1965) allows local governments to tax farms and ranches according to the income they produce, rather than the price a developer might pay for the land. In return, the owner enters into a binding contract to maintain the land in agricultural use for a minimum period of 10 years. Each year the contract is automatically renewed for another 10 years, unless a notice of non-renewal is filed by the owner or the public agency cancels the contract. This amounts to a lease of development right to the government. A total of 13,700,000 acres are currently under Williamson Act Contract. During the past three years, 37,376 acres have been non-renewed or removed, of which 5,643 acres were prime lands.

The Williamson Act, although effective in areas where it has been applied, has played a limited role in solving the interface problems between agriculture and urban growth, and the premature conversion of productive agricultural lands. It is a voluntary program and administered inconsistently throughout the state (11 of the 58 counties do not offer it at all) and it does little to guarantee the long-term preservation of productive agricultural areas.

Maintaining Agricultural Land

Because our agriculture is highly specialized, we must recognize its various special requirements as we select land for preservation—rather than merely setting aside acreage without regard for its use. Present maps showing "prime" or "potential

prime" lands were adequate to Williamson Act purposes but will not be adequate for comprehensive planning. In the future it will be necessary to define agricultural use areas on the basis of other economic, political, and enivronmental criteria.

The strength of the state's agricultural economy lies in its diversification. The special requirements of over 200 agricultural products must be recognized as lands are designated for agricultural preservation. Important work was completed by the Office of Planning and Research in 1974, identifying state-wide those land which best lend themselves to producing a wide variety of agricultural products. These "prime" and "potential prime" agricultural lands comprise 20,3000,000 acres or 20 percent of the state's total land resources.

There is no guarantee that lands actually converted to urban use are those lands best suited for urban development or that their loss would not be critical to certain specialty crops. There was common concern among the Task Force on this point, and this concern was one of the key underlying reasons for the consensus that a comprehensive state land-use planning program should be undertaken immediately.

It must be recognized that urban, agricultural and open space uses each have their own requirements. Lacking the certainty of a long-term plan for each use, as well as guidelines for transitional areas during periods of adjustment, current conflicts will continue. One of the primary values of a state land-use plan must be to reduce this uncertainty.

Reserving land for agricultural use does not automatically guarantee agricultural productivity. If the owner of the land cannot produce crops competitively—and if it

is in the public interest that crop production continue—other means may have to be employed.

Tax relief for successful production is one such incentive; subsidization from public funds is another. Buying development rights or outright purchase of the land are other ways to encourage agricultural production which is not economically competitive. Many forms of incentive-creation and/or public acquisition are available, and may in the long run have to be considered to maintain the kinds of agricultural productivity we need.

As with other aspects of California's need to plan for the future, agricultural policies must be considered on an overall basis, together with energy, water, housing, transportation, and other factors affecting the people of California.

1. Classified as Soil Classes I & II by the United States Soil Conservation Service.
2. Source: *Conservation Needs Inventory–1970*. California Soil Conservation Service.
3. *The Future of California's Agriculture 1974-2000*. Report of the Agricultural Blue Ribbon Committee. Commission for Economic Development. September 1974.
4. *A Hungry World: The Challenge to Agriculture*. Cooperative Extension, University of California, Summer 1974.
5. *The Future of California's Agriculture 1974-2000*.
6. *Facts About California Agriculture*. 1970. Agricultural Extension. University of California.
7. Prime agricultural land is defined in Section 51201 (c) of the Government Code (the Williamson Act of 1965) as; Soil Classes I and II or rated 80-100 on the Storie Index for forested areas; land planted to crops which normally return at least $200/acre/year or which have done so in three of the last five years; land which supports livestock used for the production of food and fiber.
8. Potential prime land is defined by the Department of Water Resources as "lands which have the capacity of being made prime through normal agricultural investment and practices."
9. State Department of Food and Agriculture.

FINDINGS/AGRICULTURE

1. The state should provide for the preservation of agricultural lands and their management under principles of sustained yield.

2. In addressing the agricultural land preservation issue, the members of the Task Force have been unable to agree on only one point: the time frame within which the Legislature should act to designate agricultural lands to be preserved. Therefore we present here the only place in this report where consensus was not reached. Alternate findings are shown, representing two different points of view.

Alternate A

California's agricultural lands must be preserved. The Legislature should act immediately to preserve for agricultural use all lands already defined as prime agricultural lands according to the Williamson Act. The Legislature should also adopt policies, standards, and criteria for identifying other agricultural or potential agricultural lands which should be reserved for agricultural use. The State Planning Council, as recommended in Chapter 3, should apply these policies, standards and criteria in determining which lands should be zoned for agricultural use in the State Land-Use Plan.

Alternate B

The State Land-Use Plan must be developed as a comprehensive land-use plan. Equal consideration must be given to the state's land needs for agriculture, housing, and sources of employment. The conversion of 15-20,000 acres of agricultural land per year until adoption of the state plan in 1977, considering the current state prime land inventory of 12,700,000 acres, is not sufficiently critical to require a halt to suburban development or to warrant the adoption of yet another single-purpose state plan. Such an action would be inconsistent with the other findings of the Task Force calling for a comprehensive approach to state land-use planning. Preservation policy must be combined with development policy. There must be a parallel concern for both preservation and economic growth.

3. The state should establish incentives to ensure that land within designated agricultural use areas remains in (or is developed for) agricultural use.

4. The State Council should carefully evaluate the energy, manpower, water, capital, and modern technology costs against the land resource to be sure the public receives the highest quality food at the most reasonable cost.

5. Some form of assistance should be made available to protect family-owned and operated farms which would otherwise be unable to remain in agricultural production.

6. Taxation and assessment practices should be revised so that they support the preservation of prime agricultural lands. Such lands should be taxed according to their agricultural use, provided that there is a long-term provision to keep the land in such use and a substantial penalty for conversion to non-agricultural use.

7. Within urban areas, agricultural uses such as small family farms and community garden plots should be assisted by local governments.

8. Agricultural owners should be permitted, but not required, to open their property to recreation uses which do not interfere with the land's ability to produce and which do not create undue hardship on the property owner.

4. RESOURCES

California's historical growth has always been connected with its resources—gold, timber, oil, water—and the state's prosperity today is still dependent upon its rich support system of natural resources. The things we call natural resources are mostly in and of the land, and thus land-use policy inevitably deals with the use and preservation of resources.

Resources, like the land itself, once seemed to be in limitless supply. But we can see today that tremendous increases in population and consumption throughout the years have seriously damaged and depleted much of our natural resource support system. Even if population and consumption were to remain at present levels we would be faced with critical problems of resource management.

Resources are generally classified as "renewable", "reusable", or "non-renewable". Each category presents it own problems of use and management.

Non-Renewable Resources

Fossil fuels, such as oil, natural gas and coal, are considered non-renewable because they are irreversibly converted to heat when burned to produce energy. Oil and natural gas are found in several areas in California; and their development has been inadequately controlled in the past by uncoordinated, fragmented regulatory systems. Many resource extraction decisions have been made by local governments without long-range planning, study of priorities, or a statewide concern.

It is time for the state to prepare a comprehensive plan for the use and management of non-renewable resources as part of overall land-use policy, and to see that management principles are administered by an appropriate level of government.

Costs and priorities must also be considered. The extraction of most non-renewable mineral resources has carried high energy costs and high ecological costs. The ecological costs are external to the extraction process and do not become part of the price of the commodity.

Often, the same land may have different and incompatible resource uses, such as when a mineral deposit is found in an area that is a watershed or an important wildlife habitat. In these cases, priorities must be carefully weighed before irrevocable decisions are made.

In addition, California possesses many natural areas of unique ecological importance, some of which are threatened by development. These areas must be inventoried and preserved.

Reusable Resources

Although mineral resources are not renewable, they are, in most cases, reusable. Gold is a good example of a metal that is almost always recycled and reused. Metal and glass can also be recycled, and we have barely begun to explore the possibilities for extending our reserves of non-renewable resources by recycling supplies already extracted. An intensive and systematic search for more efficient recycling and reuse of commodities should be a first priority of both government and industry.

This is closely related to solid waste disposal. There are increasing restrictions against landfill as a means of disposing of solid refuse, and the problem of finding dumping space promises to become ever more critical with diminishing open land and growing population. Some communities have already shown that an energetic

Base future use of resources on a structure of priorities to balance resource use, conservation and recovery.
(Finding 2, page 59.)

recycling program can reduce the volume of solid refuse, which would otherwise waste energy, resources, and land for disposal. Statewide land-use management logically includes coordination of regional waste management programs with policies and incentives to recycle and reuse whenever possible.

Our most valuable reusable resource is water, and land-use policy must address the conflict inherent in the demands made upon California's water resources by energy production, agriculture and urban development. Management of watersheds, flood plains, rivers and ground water resources must be integrated with traditional methods of land-use planning.

Renewable Resources

The third category of resources includes all those which live and grow and can—at least in theory—be maintained in an indefinitely replenished supply. Fish and wildlife are renewable resources. Timber and rangeland are also, and both are important to us: we depend on timber for shelter and on rangeland for food and wool. All renewable resources are dependent upon maintenance of water supplies.

California cuts more timber each year than any other state except Oregon, and our continuing consumption of this resource is based upon the concept of "sustained yield." However, there is controversy over the question of whether this policy of sustained yield is actually being followed.

Rangeland—of which California has some 10,000,000 acres—is another resource which should be managed on a sustained yield principle. Those lands are now yielding far less in forage than they might: many ranges have lost one-half to two-thirds of their livestock carrying capacity, and this is partly because of our somewhat over-zealous fire supression practices and overgrazing, which has caused soil and erosion problems. Fire—in spite of the tendency to think of it as a natural enemy—is part of the ecosystem that produces the resource.

One example of the connection between land-use planning and resource man-

**Manage public lands
in accordance with
state land-use policies.**
(Finding 6, page 59.)

agement is the interface between urban development and the management of chaparral lands. When urban development takes place in chaparral areas, some management options (such as controlled burning) are made more difficult or are completely removed.

Fire is important in the forest as well. In certain types of forest it kills off under-bush and saplings without harming trees. When natural fires are suppressed for many years the under-story growth fills with fuel; then when a fire eventually does occur it destroys both the brush and the trees.

Fire and fuel management, using natural and controlled burns as well as suppression, would enhance the quality of rangeland, chaparral and forests.

PUBLIC LANDS

Federal

Federal agencies control nearly half of California's land space, and this area contains a sizeable portion of our renewable, reusable and non-renewable resources. State and federal land-use decisions sometimes work in opposite directions. If state land-use policies are to be effective it will be necessary for federal agencies to work closely with the state toward the same goals. Lack of articulated national land-use policies will interfere with implementation of state land-use policies on federal lands in California.

State

The state itself owns some 5,500,000 acres of California. A million acres of this is in state parks, state forests, water project lands, and other properties administered by departments of the Resources Agency. Most of the state-owned property—including school lands in remote areas and some 3,500,000 acres of submerged lands—are under the control of the State Lands Commission.

The State Lands Commission has never prepared a complete inventory of state lands, and its limited powers make it difficult to manage these lands or to protect them from abuse. The present staff is small, and is mainly concerned with oil and gas leasing.

Local

State grants of "home rule" power to local governments make no mention of resource management, and in general local governments in California have concerned themselves little with resources.

However, in recent years some local governments have begun to pay more attention to the value of resource lands such as marsh lands, coastline, and open space. This response has been rather late in coming and authority in these areas has been occasionally pre-empted by specialized regional agencies such as the San Francisco Bay Conservation and Development Commission and the Coastal Zone Conservation Commissions and the Tahoe Regional Planning Agency.

Some counties have ordinances to regulate such practices as timber harvest and quarrying; but at the present time there is no clear and consistent state-wide definition of the responsibilities of local governments in regard to resource management, nor is there a state appeals process to review local decisions involving the use or protection of resources.

FINDINGS / RESOURCES

1. Provision for management of all natural resources should be an integral part of the California State Land-Use Plan.

2. The future use of resources should be based on a structure of priorities to balance resource use, conservation and recovery.

3. The state should prepare a resource management plan that will provide for:

- The wise use and protection of its non-renewable resources;
- the sustained yield of its renewable resources;
- recycling and reuse of resources.

4. A state appeals process should be established to review, and if necessary override, local decisions involving the use or protection of resources of state-wide concern.

5. New state policies should include the use of range, forest, and brush fire in its resource management programs.

6. Public lands should be managed in accordance with state land-use policies.

7. The state should urge those federal agencies which manage lands in California to conform their management to state land-use policies.

8. All state agencies with jurisdiction over state lands should be required to follow state land-use policies.

5. ENERGY

The 1973 gasoline shortage caused many difficulties and inconveniences to Californians, but in the long run this may have been healthy. It showed dramatically that cheap and unlimited energy can no longer be taken for granted. With startling speed the state adopted policies inconceivable a few years earlier: policies aimed toward energy conservation and a declining rate of growth in per capita consumption.

Some of the energy realities we now confront are:

- We are highly dependent on foreign energy sources which are beyond our direct control.
- Energy supply issues are of more than local, regional, or state-wide concern.
- The demand for energy has been increasing five times as fast as population growth, as a result of such factors as industrialization, mechanization and fertilization to increase farm production, and an energy-wasting transportation system.
- High energy use carries high environmental costs from extraction, processing, transportation, conversion, and distribution.

Although the energy crisis is a national—in fact a world-wide—problem, some aspects of it must be dealt with as matters of California land-use policy. Even if the growth of energy consumption can be contained, there will still be a need to ensure an adequate long-term supply.

The Energy Industry and Land

Our existing energy facilities—refineries, power plants, dams, tanker docks, transmission lines—are all themselves uses of the land, with various ecological costs. The extraction of resources from undeveloped land may scar it permanently or create industrial districts in unsuitable areas. Construction of new energy facilities and offshore drilling each cause public controversy. There is even growing debate over the exploitation of underground steam fields, which are often in remote and scenic surroundings. Energy facilities are usually visually unattractive—which is one kind of impact upon the area in which they are located—and they also make demands on other resources. Power plants require water for cooling and other uses, and fossil fuel plants contribute to pollution of both water and air. The storage of nuclear wastes is another complex land-use problem connected to energy supply. Transmission facilities are yet another issue requiring consideration of the ecological costs of delivering energy to consumers. Use of solar energy is developing very slowly, but its use for heating and cooling buildings should increase substantially in the near future, as it is relatively non-polluting.

Plan land use to conserve energy.
(Finding 3, page 65.)

Land-Use Patterns and Energy

It is clear that the way land is used in California is intimately connected with our consumption of energy. Present consumption is in large part the result of suburbanization of California, the quest for the single family home, and reliance on private automobiles for transportation. Several studies have shown that as density rises above a certain level, energy consumption begins to drop. This is mainly related to

**Encourage and
develop more efficient
methods of moving
people and goods.**

(Finding 5, page 65.)

transportation and suggests that more compact urban forms are more efficient energy users. California uses more energy for transportation than any other state, and 75 percent of the petroleum used in California is consumed in automobiles.

Although the climate makes it possible for California to use less energy for heating per household than other parts of the country, suburbanization has produced thousands of homes with energy-intensive appliances and a dramatic increase in the use of electricity and natural gas.

Land-use patterns produce other, less direct, effects upon energy use. When development covers agricultural land near cities, energy is wasted in several ways: replacement cropland normally requires more fertilization, more water from distant sources, and longer freight runs between the fields and the market.

The transfer of water to accomodate agriculture and urbanization in water-scarce areas also consumes a great deal of energy. Power used for pumping in the California Water Project will be a significant percentage of all electrical energy used in the state for agriculture.

Energy Cost

The spreading of cities after World War II was made possible by good roads and—more fundamentally—by cheap gasoline. If the price of gasoline had reflected its true costs, fewer people could have afforded the suburban home and the long commute.

It is evident that the abundant availability of inexpensive energy has been one cause of its high use and has reinforced the general attitude that it is in limitless supply. Energy prices have not incorporated the full social and ecological costs of its extraction, processing, conversion, and transportation; we may be paying for many years to come the overdue bills on energy.

We may also find it necessary to re-think our ways of measuring energy resources. We have traditionally calculated energy in terms of the use of non-renewable fossil fuels, and have in the process neglected to pay full attention to our vast reserves of human energy. Ironically, we find ourselves in the midst of an energy crisis and an unemployment crisis at the same time—which suggests the need for developing a more comprehensive and creative view of our total energy potential.

Planning

If land-use planning is carried on with proper attention to the need to conserve energy it will almost certainly lead to more compact urban forms. A further saving could result from mixed-use districts with shopping, employment and residences close together. In view of the many arguments against further development on the urban fringe, it may now be time to go to work full-scale on the revitalization of the inner cities.

Since transportation accounts for 30 percent of all energy needs, transportation systems must be planned with energy conservation in mind. In the recent past we have become increasingly reliant on high energy-consumption systems: the automobile for the commuter, the truck for the commercial shipper, the airplane for the intercity traveler. Comprehensive planning with expanded surface public transportation offers an opportunity to reduce energy costs overall.

The Energy Agency

The State Energy Resources Conservation and Development Act of 1974 made it state policy to "employ a range of measures to reduce wasteful, uneconomical and unnecessary uses of energy, thereby reducing the rate of growth of energy consumption, prudently conserve energy resources, and assure statewide environmental, public safety and land-use goals"; and established a new Energy Resources Conservation and Development Commission.

In theory, the Commission will have nothing to do with land-use planning. In practice, it will have a great deal to do with it. Two of its duties are directly related to land use:

- It will prepare a binding plan for California, forecast electrical energy demand, and determine what level of demand should be satisfied in order to balance environmental protection with other needs.
- The Commission will decide what electric generating facilities are to be built and where. In the past, power plant proposals required the consent of at least a dozen federal agencies, 15 state agencies, city and county agencies and other special purpose agencies; they will now be certified in a single proceeding by the Energy Commission. Though some state agencies must still add their approval, local governments have advisory powers only and cannot veto.

Like other state agencies which have broad powers and a narrowly-defined purpose, the new Energy Commission has not been given an essential tool that it needs: a comprehensive state-wide land-use policy to guide it.

State land-use policies will be based in part on the need to conserve energy. These must be established soon so that the Energy Resources Conservation and Development Commission can relate its decisions to the state land-use plan.

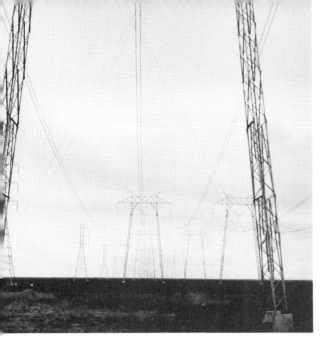 

FINDINGS/ENERGY

1. The availability of energy and the siting of facilities to supply energy both help to determine how the land is used.

2. Land-use patterns influence the energy consumption in a region. Jobs and homes should be close to reduce travel distance. Compact urban forms may exhibit a high efficiency in the use of energy and should be considered for their possible environmental and social costs.

3. Land use must be planned to conserve energy.

4. Practices to curb the wasteful use of energy should be implemented by the newly created Energy Resources Conservation and Development Commission.

5. Transportation in California is the largest energy consumer. There should be a system of incentives and disincentives to encourage and develop more efficient methods of moving people and goods.

6. Research into environmentally inexpensive sources of energy should be greatly increased, together with research into energy-saving principles of planning and design.

7. Energy costs in the past have not reflected the true environmental and social costs associated with extraction, processing, conversion, and transmission of energy. These costs should be incorporated in the overall price of energy. State policies should assure that all segments of society receive subsistence energy to meet basic needs for food and shelter.

8. As required by AB 1575 (1974) and recent amendments to the California Environmental Quality Act, state, areawide, and local land-use plans, as well as plans for specific projects, must now consider mitigation measures to minimize the wasteful, inefficient, and unnecessary consumption of energy.

9. The planning of energy facilities must be closely coordinated with state land-use policies.

6. TRANSPORTATION

Transportation systems—roads and railroads, ports and airports—have shaped the use of land in California and will continue to shape it in the future. Transportation is perhaps the most important of the many forces that must be understood in developing land-use policy.

Patterns of change in urban and rural areas are affected by the available transportation systems which provide access to jobs, schools, and other goods and services. A decision to build a new freeway or a public transportation facility has a major impact upon the future growth of the area it serves.

The first cities in California—as in other parts of the world—grew up around harbors, and subsequent growth was helped along by other transit systems such as the railroad and the street car. Then came the automobile, which provided fast, private, even luxurious personal mobility. Californians adopted it with enthusiasm and the automobile has shaped our landscape and lifestyles.

Dependence upon the automobile was encouraged by government plans and policies. There was a state freeway master plan and a federal interstate highway program, and ambitious local road and highway plans as well. Boulevard-wide streets were required in new developments. State and federal highway trust funds guaranteed ample financing from gasoline tax receipts.

The spread of the automobile was never thought of as a way of developing land use, except by those local governments which encouraged highways to promote growth. The car was simply seen as one element in the Great American Dream in which everyone could own a home on a 6,000 square foot lot. People wanted mobility, better living conditions, more land, and cleaner and safer environments. So the cities spread out, and the personal car was the transportation system that made it possible.

The impact of all the new roads and highways was never seriously considered. Yet the automobile was shaping the landscape, creating patterns of growth utterly different from any seen before. It was also filling our skies with smog, which became a serious health problem in many California communities.

Now our cities are widespread, built at low densities, covering hills and fields. The central element in them is the commuter, some of whom drive 50 or even 100 miles a day. A recent SCAG report on transportation indicates that the average home to work vehicle trip is slightly longer than 10 miles. It also notes that of the total trips made on an average weekday, 88.4 percent are made by personal auto and only 2.2 percent by bus.[10]

Although jobs have also moved out of the center city, they have moved more slowly. People who do not own cars often find it hard to get around, even in areas served by public transportation. Mass transit systems are designed for commuters, but in areas of low density housing it is hard to compete with the automobile. Workers who have to drive to get to a transit station tend to drive on past it. Many transit systems have either been abandoned or have deteriorated through neglect.

Reliance on the automobile involves a lavish waste of energy, with a cost that was invisible so long as gasoline was cheap. And the matter was made more serious by a parallel development: an increasing dependence upon highway transportation of cargo. Nearly half the money spent on transportation in the U.S. in 1970 went to move cargo, and the bulk of that—$70 billion out of $90 billion—was for trucking.

In the 1960s, people began to ask questions about the direction in which the

Integrate transportation planning with land-use planning at all levels of government.

(Finding 3, page 71.)

Establish state land-use policies before the final California Transportation Plan is adopted by the Legislature.

(Finding 5, page 71.)

commitment to the automobile was taking us. By 1970, the need to abandon the commitment was apparent—but policies and institutions which perpetuate the automobile are resistant to change.

The State Transportation Plan

In 1972 the state Legislature changed a number of rules for transportation planning. It established a new Department of Transportation—Caltrans—which reports to a State Transportation Board. The Division of Highways was organized within the new department along with the other offices of Aeronautics, Mass Transportation and Transportation Planning.

The Division of Transportation Planning must carry out the Legislature's most important charge to Caltrans: preparation of a new California Transportation Plan. This plan, which will be submitted to the Legislature in 1976, must:

- Be "Balanced" and "multi-modal". That is, it must give a prominent place to transportation systems other than the private car.
- Provide for environmental protection and serve social goals.
- Offer alternatives to the private car for people who do not or cannot drive.
- Weigh the effect of transportation decisions on land use.
- Be accompanied by an environmental impact report.

The plan is to be built from the lower levels up. The basic work will be done by various local or regional agencies: two agencies of regional government, three region-wide councils of governments, and several single-county COGs or local transportation commissions. At the state level, the Division of Transportation will take these area plans and combine them, recommending changes where they conflict with each other or with state guidelines. The State Transportation Board will review the combined plan and forward it to the Legislature.

The state plan and each of the area plans will be discussed in an environmental impact report. The law also sets up procedures for public participation in the planning process.

However, there are problems built into the 1972 law which may threaten the value of the completed plan. Among these are the following:

Time ● The entire project of preparing a statewide transportation plan—something which has never been attempted before—is to be completed within three years. Recent progress reports indicate that the plan submitted to the Legislature in 1976 will be a very preliminary version: that, in fact, it will be unfinished.

Money ● In the 1973-74 fiscal year the Division of Transportation Planning had a budget of $13.6 million—of which $9 million, transferred from the Division of Highways, can by law be spent on highway planning only. The 1974-75 budget was slightly higher, but is still inadequate for public transportation planning and implementation.

"Bottoms-up" planning ● There are certain disadvantages to a planning process which initiates with local agencies. We cannot assume that the local agencies will take a sufficiently broad view of the state's transportation needs, and that they will take seriously state guidelines which do not have legal force. It is true that the state

board can amend the regional plans and that the Division of Transportation planning has ongoing contact with the local agencies—but there remains a fundamental difference between a patchwork of local plans and a single plan constructed with the entire state in mind.

Absence of land-use policy ● This is the most crucial problem of all. We know from experience that transportation affects land use. And this raises the question of whether we can formulate an adequate transportation plan if there is no explicit land-use policy to guide it. Caltrans planners are instructed to make their plans conform to the land-use planning supposedly being done in the Office of Planning and Research. However, OPR has not in fact undertaken any state-wide land-use planning. In its absence, transportation planning assumes an authority it was not meant to have. In its progress report of April 1974, the Caltrans staff commented: "because there is no process that considers impacts, resources, and priorities for the entire state, the California Transportation Plan could become a de facto land-use plan for the state."

The November 1974 Progress Report further underscores the absence of a comprehensive state land-use plan: "It is generally acknowledged that transportation is intended to support and complement higher order social needs. These needs are most effectively addressed and expressed through comprehensive land-use plans. To date, no such plan exists at the state level."

Difficulty of implementing multi-modal plans ● Although Caltrans is now officially committed to balanced planning, it is still easier to implement highway programs or transit projects intended to serve the commuter than it is to create other kinds of transportation. Most of the money still goes to highways, and Caltrans has no jurisdiction over ports, airports, or transit providers. Ninety percent of Caltrans employees work in the Division of Highways. Proposition 5, approved by California voters in June 1974, is the state's first major effort toward funding public transportation systems. The Act amended Article 26 of the State Constitution to permit the use of a limited share of gas tax revenues for mass transit.

Give top priority to the development of multi-modal public transportation systems.

(Finding 6, page 71.)

The California Department of Transportation has estimated that $807.6 million in Article 26 revenues will be available for mass transit purposes for the five year period of 1975/76 through 1979/80. Los Angeles County will be eligible for $208.1 million; San Francisco, $15.7 million; San Diego, $54 million.

Each of these problems cited above can be overcome by a clear state-level commitment to land-use planning and to multi-modal transportation planning and funding in support of it. If a State Transportation Plan is adopted by the Legislature before state land-use policies and guidelines are adopted, the Transportation Plan will preempt sound state land-use planning and transportation and development may continue to proceed in directions the state no longer desires.

10. Preliminary Regional Transportation Plan, Southern California Association of Governments, January 1975.

FINDINGS/TRANSPORTATION

1. Transportation systems determine, in part, the nature and location of development. They affect the use of energy and the quality of the environment, particularly air quality.

2. The expansion of transportation systems without adequate regard for long-range land-use planning often encourages undesirable patterns of land use.

3. Therefore, transportation planning should be integrated with land-use planning at all levels of government.

4. California transportation planning and land-use policies must be developed concurrently and result in integrated implementation programs.

5. State land-use policies should be established before the final California Transportation Plan is adopted by the Legislature. If the California Transportation Plan is acceptable to the Legislature, it should be adopted in 1976 as an interim plan only.

6. The development of multi-modal public transportation systems must be given top priority at all levels of government.

7. State, regional, and local transportation agencies must be given adequate funds for the planning and implementation of multi-modal public transportation systems.

8. Such systems should reduce California's dependency on the private automobile, encourage more efficient use of all modes of transportation, encourage people to live near their work, and provide for convenient short and non-commute trips.

9. Until there is a California Transportation Plan based on state land-use policies, transportation projects should be critically examined for their possible implications for air quality, energy consumption, and the course of development.

7. TAXATION

Taxation does two things: It brings in revenue, and it regulates. The first was the original reason for imposing taxes, but now the public and government officials realize that taxation works also as a tool of public policy; it can affect the way people act, by making some actions more expensive than others.

Both functions of taxation influence the use of the land, often in ways that were not anticipated and are not consistent with California's present needs.

Taxation as Revenue

Actually, few citizens are even aware of the relationship between the demands they place on a community and the taxes levied by the community to provide those services.

Real property taxes were designed to pay the cost of services furnished to the property and the people of a community. In general, the tax rates will be higher in a community which has a high level of services—except where there are other sources of city or county revenue such as high sales tax returns from regional shopping centers or taxes on mineral rights.

Real property taxes are determined by the independent actions of two separate bodies of government. A County Assessor's office independently sets values to be assigned to specific parcels of land and improvements thereon. A different body—city council or county board of supervisors—sets a rate of taxation. Therefore a specific jurisdiction's revenue results from assessed valuation times the tax rate, and this must relate to its budget for public services.

The revenue from property taxes is abundant in some areas and sparse in others. Commercial and industrial properties yield the most; residential properties are comparatively unprofitable because the tax collected does not offset the necessary services such as fire and police protection, roads, waste treatment, and schools. Many communities have found that only expensive housing yields more than it consumes.

So, local jurisdictions have competed for industrial and commercial development. Some officials have talked of preventing residential development which does not have a "cost-benefit ratio" in the government's favor. This is understandable, but it could have disastrous results; planning by dollar benefit to an individual community can aggravate regional and state-wide land-use problems. Low-income citizens have to live and obtain public services somewhere.

One ingenious response to this problem has been used by the limited regional government in the Twin Cities Metropolitan Area of Minnesota. It is a program of regional revenue sharing: a percentage of the assessed valuation of new commercial and industrial development is treated as a regional tax base. The revenue is distributed back to local governments by a formula which gives most to the areas where the local tax base is weakest.

Public works programs present another revenue issue related to land-use policy. Expensive projects often drive up the value of properties they serve, but these properties seldom help pay for the projects. For example, the Bay Bay Area Rapid Transit System has added an estimated $1 billion to the sale price of property in the communities it serves—but the system itself is financed by the sales tax. Some planners favor the use of a tax to recover some of the value added to property by public works and use it to finance the projects.

Make state and local taxation policy support state land-use policies and goals.
(Finding 1, page 75.)

Initiate a thorough study by the Legislature of the entire tax structure and its effects on land use.

(Finding 2, page 75.)

It has long been obvious that differences in revenue among districts resulted in variations in the quality of public services. In California, the State Supreme Court has ruled in the case of *Serrano vs. Priest* that this inequity as relates to public education violates the doctrine of equal protection under the law. As a result of this decision the Legislature must find a way to equalize the tax support for public education, and this may result in a system of financing education on a state-wide basis and from sources other than the property tax. Again, this reform would have a major impact on land-use patterns.

Taxation as Regulation

The power to tax is a source of power to control how land is used. Unfortunately, this has not always been clearly understood by taxing authorities; the result has been taxation which was intended to be merely revenue-producing but which had regulatory effects that were both unexpected and undesirable.

Taxation and assessment policies have clearly contributed to the loss of California farmland. Near an expanding urban area, farmland may sell at several times its agricultural value. Because developers must bid high in order to persuade the first owners to cash in on their land, the price of parcels may be far higher than its real value for development. This artificial price then becomes the basis for assessed valuation and thus for the property tax. These high taxes encourage owners to sell.

One alternative is to use the taxing power to encourage retention of farmland in agricultural use—by taxing it according to the income it actually produces rather than its value for development. The Williamson Act was California's first experiment with this method of taxation, and a step in the right direction. However, it is now time to explore the possibility of a complete revision of taxes on rural lands as a part of land-use policy.

We should also consider how changes in taxation policy might contribute to the restoration of old urban areas. Under present practices taxes increase quickly whenever an owner builds something on his land or rebuilds or improves existing structures. But vacant land or land with run-down buildings is lightly taxed—thus it pays an owner to permit decay. But a revised structure, with light taxes on improvements, could create an incentive to private redevelopment.

Taxation of standing timber is also a regulatory power. Under present law, the timberland owner must begin paying taxes when his trees are 40 years old. Therefore, many owners decide to cut in the 41st year. However, 40 years is not enough time to mature timber for some uses. Timber companies and landowners that might prefer to wait longer before cutting choose to harvest in order to avoid years of extra tax. The solution appears to be tax timber when cut, not before; this would be a tax on yield, not on inventory. The same approach may well apply to other resources.

In general, the shortcomings of past taxation and assessment methods appear to result not so much from mistaken policy as from a lack of policy and a disregard for the regulatory impacts of taxes. The development of a basic land-use policy is the main recommendation of this report; we also recommend intensive study of the effects of the tax system so that it may be used knowingly and intelligently in support of that policy.

REAL PROPERTY APPRAISAL INFORMATION

74

FINDINGS/TAXATION

1. State and local taxation policy should be supportive of state land-use policies and goals.

2. The California Legislature should make a thorough, well-publicized, and authoritative study of the entire tax structure and its effects on the use of the land.

3. Among the questions to be considered in such a study are:

- Should major public works—such as highways or waste treatment plants—which permit more intense utilization of land be paid for in greater part by some method of installment taxes, bonds or liens by the residents of the area receiving the primary benefits of the public improvement?

- Should a method of land taxation be applied to the inner city so that a parcel's location, not the improvements constructed on it, becomes the major factor in determining its tax?

- Should timber be taxed at the time of harvest, rather than before? Should the assessment and taxation of resources generally be on an inventory and severance basis?

- Should farmland be taxed according to the income it is producing, without regard for its value for development?

- In metropolitan regions, should a portion of the tax base brought in by new commercial and industrial development be shared among local governments?

- Is the increased increment to property value, brought about by public improvements, sufficiently taxed and properly shared?

- Should assessment appeals boards adjust property taxes to reflect actual use rather than possible or speculative future use?

- Should property taxes generally be reduced and more of the burden shifted to income, business, sales and other taxes?

- If public education is financed state-wide and from sources other than the property tax, how will development pressures on land use be affected?

4. All levels of government should work to educate the public about the relationship between government budgets (which provide services to the people) and property taxes (which pay, in large part, for those services).

8. COMPENSATION

At any public hearing where development is the issue, in any session of the Legislature, in any planning study group, debates about land-use controls quickly focus on this question: When the use of a piece of land is restricted, should compensation be paid to the owner? This is a complex issue, related to our fundamental beliefs about what it means to own land.

Concepts of Land Ownership

The traditional concept of land ownership in our society has viewed land as a commodity. Under this view, land in private ownership exists to be used to private advantage. Government should not unduly interfere with the owner's freedom to make a profit and should restrict use of the land only for public health and safety reasons and to prevent injury to other property or persons. The right to develop is part of the land itself, and cannot be too much restricted without compensating the owner for his loss.

An alternative concept views land as a resource, semipublic in nature; the best use of it may be no developed use at all. Government regulation is seen as necessary to protect public interests in the use of land, and the property owner's right to develop is regarded as a privilege created and granted by the government in order to insure and perpetuate its use for the public good.

Today the "resource" concept appears to be replacing the "commodity" concept as it becomes more widely understood that development of land has far-reaching social and ecological impacts. However, the matter is not simply one of changing attitudes; it is complicated by the nature of land ownership. There are, of course, large land holdings by individuals and corporations whose purpose of ownership is not personal use but investment and resale. There are also similar land investments by labor union pension funds, teacher retirement funds, university endowment funds, and others. A large segment of our population, in short, has an interest in land as a "commodity."

Landowners are uncertain as to how much regulation of land-use in the public interest can or will occur without government compensation to the owner. Owners of individual lots in particular are likely to believe they are entitled to compensation for any loss in development opportunity.

Litigation on this issue—and there has been much of it—has typically centered around the "taking clause" of the Fifth Amendment to the United States Constitution, which states: ". . . nor shall private property be taken for public use without just compensation."[11]

The Taking Clause in California

California courts have been inclined to give great weight to public purpose, allowing regulation a great deal of scope. This tendency has increased with the recent rush of laws and ordinances designed to protect the environment and conserve resources. Particularly in the last decade, California courts have repeatedly upheld the validity of strict land-use regulations and controls even when they have substantially decreased market value in the land when a public purpose is served.

Relate use of the police power to clearly described public benefits, and make regulation consistent with adopted state and regional comprehensive planning goals.
(Finding 2, page 80.)

Nevertheless, many land-use decisions by public officials have been influenced by the fear that a particular regulation might be judged in the courts to have gone "too far".

It now seems likely that the California Supreme Court will sustain the constitutionality of land-use restrictions which are based on at least one of the following:

- Legislative declarations of public intent and policy clarifying the purpose served and general plan elements, standards, and implementing ordinances.
- Considerations of regional (or more than local) scope.

For example, the Court has been firm in upholding the authority of the Tahoe Regional Planning Agency, the Bay Conservation and Development Commission, and the Coastal Commission.

Inequities

The transition has been difficult, especially for property owners who have not understood the extent of it. Many land-owners have staked a great deal on "inevitable" development. Owners of individual lots have suffered unexpected economic hardship, particularly when their land is downzoned. Often they had been sold the land with the promise that they cannot lose—and can expect to profit—from land purchases. Because many people mistakenly believe that landowners are entitled to compensation wherever government restriction causes loss in land value there have been many disappointments and much litigation.

The compensation issue is related to the market value of land, and this has contributed to the difficulty of the transition. There are many areas in California where zoning regulations established legal density standards which were both environmentally and economically unrealistic. Such "overzoning", however, is not a valid standard for determining whether compensation should be paid when the area is properly zoned. Perceived market values have sometimes been based upon unrealistic expectations, and even the valuation of land by a tax assessor may involve much guesswork as to what use may be approved and whether such uses may be the basis for sound investment. Where there is to be compensation, it should not be based on a market value inflated by unrealistic expectation.

Remedies

Although the "taking issue" is appropriate for judicial determination, other compensation issues should not be left solely to the courts, but must be dealt with as a political problem. We seek a process wherein differing interests and ideas will be heard and result in clear and authoritative legislation.

When regulations which are deemed to be for the public good place an inequitable burden on a particular landowner, some means should be found to ease the economic hardship. We suggest several possible approaches in findings to this chapter, and further urge the creation of a commission specifically charged with the task of beginning the search for new methods of compensation without delay. We encourage the search for new ideas and new ways of reducing inequities resulting from regulation of land use.

The Legislature should separate the land-use planning function from the search

Encourage open political discussion of compensation issues.

(Finding 5, page 80.)

Establish a separate commission to study compensation.

(Finding 6, page 81.)

78

for ways of dealing with economic inequities that might result from it. This is a matter of priorities as well as of Constitutional principle. The urgency of protecting important California land resources requires that the Legislature not wait for development of new concepts of compensation before establishing effective land-use policies.

We also encourage attention to the need for due process and for separation of functions: in land-use law as in other fields of law, the same people should not make the rules, enforce the rules, and then decide whether the rules are reasonable in practice.

---

11. Similar language is contained in Article I, Section 14 of the California Constitution: "Private property shall not be taken or damaged for public use without just compensation having first been made to, or paid into court for, the owner . . ."

Proceed immediately with the development of land-use policies.

(Finding 7, page 81.)

FINDINGS/COMPENSATION

1. The California law on compensation, as set forth in the California Constitution (Article I, section 14) and as interpreted by California courts, should be the basis for public land-use planning regulation.

2. In enacting state land-use policies and developing the State Land-Use Plan, care should be taken to relate use of the police power to clearly described public benefits. Regulation must be consistent with adopted state and regional comprehensive planning goals.

3. The California Supreme Court has upheld public land-use regulations which have substantially decreased the market value of the land involved. Therefore, it is not realistic for landowners to assume that they are legally entitled to compensation when government regulation reduces current market value.

4. Nevertheless, despite the general validity of land-use regulations which may reduce the market value of land, many government agencies and decision makers are hesitant to impose such regulations. Compromises result, and such compromises have many times satisfied neither landowner interests nor public planning goals sought to be implemented.

5. The Task Force believes that compensation is also a political problem, and therefore urges the Governor and Legislature to take the following action:

- Inform the public about the scope, purposes and limitations of the police power under the Constitution, including the fact that the use of the power is changing, as the needs of society change.
- Study the economic and social consequences of land-use and environmental regulations to determine under what circumstances some new forms of compensation should be provided to the landowner. This should be done in connection with the various tax and assessment studies recommended elsewhere in this report, and should include factual data about funding practices and methods now used by government agencies and decision makers.

6. Should the Legislature and Governor determine that public land-use regulation and planning has resulted (or may result) in a need for additional methods of compensation to land owners, they should establish a special commission to report back to the Legislature as soon as possible on ways to alleviate inequities to landowners from present or proposed regulations, taking into account the long-term public benefits. This commission should be independent of the State Land-Use Council recommended in this report, but there should be close communication between them and their studies should be pursued concurrently. Such a commission should study the following areas, among others:

- Creation of land development rights which could be sold and transferred from one parcel of property to another.
- Means of spreading the risk of loss due to stringent regulations by the use of an insurance concept, recognizing that at least initially the risk of loss might have to be partially underwritten by government.
- The need and techniques for recapturing benefits conferred by publicly-funded general improvements which increase the value of private land.
- More consistent criteria and an orderly process for determining what share of public costs or what degree of public subsidy is to be either imposed or granted upon specific land development projects.
- The possible creation of public, private or semi-public corporations to consolidate land ownership and, in appropriate cases, resubdivide, lease land, acquire easement and interest in land, and contract with other public agencies and private investors to accomplish specific public goals.
- Establishment of means for challenging the fairness or reasonableness of particular land-use regulations, as a separate matter from a claim of inverse condemnation.
- The extent of overzoning and methods of correction, without necessarily providing compensation.
- Density transfer rights.

7. State land-use policies and guidelines and development of the state land-use plan should not be delayed to await the results of studies outlined above, or any other studies or actions.

Chapter Three

PLANNING FOR CALIFORNIA'S FUTURE

At several points in this report we have commented upon the absence of—and the need for—a unified land-use planning process for California. In this final chapter we turn to the details of that proposal, and outline a timetable and organizational structure for such a process. Before we proceed to these specific recommendations, we wish to suggest also some general guidelines:

First, the state must decide not only what lands are suitable for policies of preservation and conservation but also what lands are suitable for policies of development. There should be explicitly stated goals for needed construction. Merely negative or restrictive land-use policies are not enough.

Controls on land use must be guided by an articulate set of goals and policies that make it clear what patterns of land use are desired and why. These should specify economic, social, physical and environmental objectives for the present and long-term future and should set priorities among these objectives. Land-use plans must address social problems which lie outside the strict definition of "land use."

Planning is an integral part of government at all levels. It must be area-wide as well as state-wide and local.

Land-use plans must be binding, first of all, on the actions of state government. State agencies have done much to shape land use by their spending policies and their decisions on what to build and what not to build. State agencies should be required to operate in accordance with a state land-use plan, and this alone would be an enormous step forward.

State planning must consider all the land. We do not support the "critical area" approach to state planning. All parts of the state are interrelated to some extent and state policy must consider the entire land area. This does not mean that the state itself must directly regulate every acre, but a policy which judges only certain lands to be "critical" and therefore worthy of state attention is inadequate.

When planning procedures and controls are established, the Legislature must appropriate the money to make them work. This may seem obvious, but in the past there have been many dramatic reforms that have failed because of inadequate financial support.

The planning process should be decision-oriented and controls must be clear. Each planning job should be assigned to some level of government with specific accountability and responsibility. There should be procedures for quick and fair

RECOMMENDATIONS

decisions when land-use conflicts arise. Explicit standards should be set so that all interested parties can be reasonably sure of where they stand.

The Governor must be involved in the planning process. The plan should reflect current policies and result in appropriate executive actions.

The Legislature must be involved in the planning process; it should create the necessary land-use planning structures and provide appropriate policy guidance on a continuing basis.

Citizens must be involved in the planning process. The plan should reflect the needs and aspirations of people, and there should be suitable channels of communication established to facilitate public participation.

The state should also maintain a statewide bank of data on land-use planning as public information, available and easy to use.

We turn now to specific recommendations for creation of a land-use planning structure. The changes proposed here are major ones, but they are also, we believe, the minimum. We must also move quickly; by doing so we may be able to avoid the bitterness and confusion that would come with fragmented controls and changes forced upon us by acute energy shortages, food crises, severe pollution and public outcry against environmental deterioration. Undoubtedly some of the planning reforms we propose should have begun long before now. But now, at least, we are operating from a greater general awareness of the nature of the problem. If we use that awareness, and accept the opportunity that we now have, we may still be able to act before the problems that we face today have turned into insoluble crises.

NEEDED ACTION

1 **1. Comprehensive land-use planning should be a top priority of the new Administration and of the Legislature.**

2 **2. In 1975 the Legislature should set in motion a comprehensive statewide land-use planning process. This is the most important issue in California today. Two important specialized plans—the Coastal Zone Conservation Plan and the California Transportation Plan—will be presented to the Legislature in early 1976; this timing reinforces the need for a statewide comprehensive planning effort.**

3 **3. The state planning process should be created in stages. The Legislature should:**

- **in 1975, establish and fund a State Land-Use Council and staff, together with interim guidelines on which it can base the exercise of its immediate powers.**
- **in 1977, adopt a state land-use plan.**
- **in 1978, create comprehensive areawide land-use planning agencies for the natural geographical regions of the state.**

RECOMMENDATIONS

GOALS

4. Apparent conflicts between environmental enhancement and economic growth can be reconciled by comprehensive land-use planning, for wise land-use decisions will both preserve the quality of the environment and provide for orderly development. State planning should provide more certainty on which land owners can rely. **4**

5. State planning should focus on the long-range results of actions taken now, emphasizing both long-term environmental impact and long-term economic costs and benefits. **5**

6. Land-use legislation should integrate environmental, social, and economic policies for the long-term benefit of all the people. **6**

DIVISION OF RESPONSIBILITY

7. The state should make planning decisions only on those land-use matters which are of major statewide importance. Certain other questions should be decided on an area-wide planning level. Most planning decisions will continue to be made at the local level. **7**

8. Area-wide planning should take place within the frame-work of state planning guidelines and should conform with state land-use policies and standards. Similarly, local planning decisions should be made within the framework of state and regional planning guidelines. **8**

9. Planning must be a two-way process. On the one hand, the state land-use plan and the area-wide plan should be binding on lower levels of government. On the other hand, both the state and the area-wide agencies should fully consider information and recommendations from the level below and recognize the importance of local land-use decision-making in the overall planning process. **9**

10. There must be a separation of functions: In land-use law as in other fields of law, the same people should not make the rules, enforce the rules, and then decide whether the rules are reasonable in practice. **10**

THE STATE LAND-USE COUNCIL

11. There should be created a State Land-Use Council to coordinate the land-use planning of all state departments and agencies and to develop a comprehensive state land-use plan. **11**

    The membership and duties of the council will be defined by the Legislature. However, we strongly suggest the following:

RECOMMENDATIONS

Structure of the State Land-Use Council

A. Five members, appointed by the Governor and confirmed by the Senate to four-year, staggered terms. All will serve full-time; one, appointed by the Governor as Chairman, will serve as a Secretary of Cabinet rank.

B. The Council must be given the staff and funding necessary to carry out its assigned tasks.

C. There should be a citizens' advisory group composed of 15 members appointed by the Governor, and broadly representative of various segments of the population.

Functions of the Council

A. To prepare the state land-use plan—in accord with legislatively determined objectives, policies, and standards—for adoption by the Legislature.

B. To enforce land-use policies pending legislative approval of the state land-use plan.

C. To guide and coordinate the land-use planning and projects of, and to resolve conflicts among, all state agencies and departments, commencing immediately.

D. The Council should likewise review the annual state budget to determine whether or not programs and projects are in accord with state land-use policies. An annual report shall be made to the Legislature, the Governor, and the people.

E. To maintain the state-wide data bank.

State Policies and Guidelines

A. Because the Council will begin its work of coordinating state planning immediately, it is important that the Legislature establish policies and guidelines on which to base the Council's decisions.

B. Among these guidelines should be some basic objectives, policies, and standards adopted by the Legislature in 1975 concerning:

- the preservation of agricultural lands;
- confining urban growth to existing urbanized areas and other areas specifically designated as suitable for new growth;
- the integration of transportation planning with state land-use policies;
- protection of the state's unique natural resources and resource areas;
- assuring area-wide distribution of an adequate housing supply;
- encouraging energy efficiency in buildings, transportation systems and land-use patterns;

RECOMMENDATIONS

● the revitalization of California's cities.

The State Land-Use Plan

A. It is to be developed by the State Land-Use Council and submitted to the Legislature in 1977. After adoption by the Legislature, the Council will review and update the plan and resubmit it to the Legislature at least every two years.

B. The Council must involve the public in its planning work through public hearings, information meetings, publicity, and by any other available means.

C. The State Land-Use Plan should contain:
   1. Identification of land in several categories:
      a.) Agricultural lands.

      b.) Boundaries of existing or potential areas which are suitable for residential (urban) growth.

      c.) Natural resource areas, such as wetlands and coastlines, to be preserved; and nonrenewable resources, such as minerals and oil, which should be conserved.

      d.) Renewable resources, such as forests and water supplies, which require careful state management.

   2. Recommended regulations and procedures to guide the proper protection or development of these areas.

   3. A long-term implementation program.

   4. Resource management standards for resource conservation areas.

   5. Recommended land-use policies for achieving federal and state noise, water, and air quality standards.

   6. A mapping of geographical regions in which area-wide planning agencies should be established, together with recommendations for the structure and authority of such agencies.

   7. A strategy for assisting in the revitalization of California's cities.

   8. Policies in regard to taxation and compensation.

   9. Recommendations for further modifications in the organization of state government which might be needed to facilitate comprehensive land-use planning.

   10. Recommended planning procedures at the state, area-wide, and local level must adhere to the basic standards of due process, proper notice and adequate opportunity to be heard.

RECOMMENDATIONS

The Land-Use Council and Other State Agencies

A. The Council should absorb the Office of Planning and Research and the Council on Intergovernmental Relations.

B. All other state agencies (including BCDC, TRPA, CCZCC, and ERCDC) should be required to submit their plans, programs, and projects to the Council for review.

C. The Council shall establish a process for resolving conflicts between projects and programs of other state agencies and the State Land-Use Plan or legislatively adopted policies and guidelines.

D. The Council should review federal policies which affect land-use in California, publicize its conclusions, and seek to coordinate federal programs with state policies.

E. The Council shall be the state agency which exercises such control or permit authority as determined proper by the Legislature in 1975 or later in order to implement the legislatively determined policies and guidelines.

AREA-WIDE PLANNING

We have sketched a broad new role for the state in land-use planning. Nevertheless, the task force feels that most land-use decisions are best made at the local or regional level—the level of government best equipped to deal with the particular land-use problem. The planning process we recommend both encourages and assists local and regional planning agencies in implementing state land-use policies and guidelines. The actual structure and responsibility of regional agencies should be developed by the State Land-Use Council, following the guidelines contained in the 1975 Legislation, and reported to the Legislature as part of its State Land-Use Plan.

12 12. Certain problems related to land use—such as air quality, water quality, transportation, solid waste management, and housing—transcend local government boundaries. Their solution must involve area-wide planning agencies.

13 13. Comprehensive area-wide planning councils should be created by the Legislature in 1978 based on the recommendations of the State Land-Use Council contained in the State Land-Use Plan. The organization and membership of the area-wide councils should be determined by the Legislature, based on the State Council's recommendations and in consultation with local governments and with existing area-wide organizations. The councils may be differently composed from region to region, but at least some members should be directly elected and the organization and responsibilities should be generally parallel to that of the State Land-Use Council.

The State Council shall designate an area-wide planning council for each of the

RECOMMENDATIONS

regions delineated in the State Land-Use Plan. Their boundaries should be logical, reflecting geography and communities of interest and not necessarily follow county lines.

14. The area-wide planning council should be charged with preparing a comprehensive regional plan including area-wide goals and policies, programs for carrying out state policies, standards for development and resource management in the region, and enforcement provisions. Elements should deal with transportation, air quality, water quality and supply, solid waste, agriculture, parks, open space, recreation areas, inner city revitalization, and adequate housing and employment centers.

14

15. Each regional plan must conform with the state land-use plan. At the same time, information gathered by the area councils, and their recommendations to the state, should be drawn upon by the State Land-Use Council in its review and update of the state land-use plan.

15

16. The area-wide council should have the authority to resolve area-wide land-use conflicts among local jurisdictions. It may also hear and decide appeals from local planning decisions, provided that such appeals are based on evidence that a local action does not conform with the regional plan.

16

LOCAL GOVERNMENT

17. Most planning decisions today are made at the local level, and that is the way it should be.

17

It is the local government, in the end, which sets the life-style in communities. Certain functions are by their nature local. In almost every other area local government must have an important share of responsibility. In the matter of low and moderate income housing, for example, an area-wide planning council would indicate quantities to be constructed and allocate equitable distribution among different parts of the urban area, based on carrying capacity and need. Among other things, local boards and councils would continue to set bulk, height, design, density, and distribution within the community.

18. Local planning must be done in the framework of area-wide planning, just as area planning must follow the state land-use plan. Recommendations and information from local governments should be one of the primary elements of any area-wide plan.

18

19. The task force recommends some reorganization of local jurisdictions. County boundaries should be changed where these are markedly at variance with geographical divisions. Many special districts should either be consolidated into local government or made part of the area-wide agencies.

19

APPENDIX

The members of the California Land-Use Task Force heard from a number of speakers, authorities in various areas of land use planning. Many of their specific points and recommendations have been incorporated into our own proposals and will already have been encountered by the reader elsewhere in this report. But, to give a more accurate account of the nature of their input, we present a brief summary of each individual's remarks to the Task Force.

William K. Reilly
Washington, D. C.
President, The Conservation Foundation
Editor, *The Use of Land*

"There is a new mood in America." So begins *The Use of Land*, the landmark 1973 report of the Rockefeller-sponsored Task Force on Land-Use and Urban Growth.

This "New Mood" is a broad popular reaction against decades of mismanaged growth: "a weariness," says Reilly, "with change itself."

- "New Mooders" demand more government control of the use of land.
- At the same time they insist that the public be more involved in government decision-making.
- They rebel against high taxes—and against developments which are held to lead to tax increases.
- They are willing to take extreme positions for bargaining purposes.
- They insist that development be of higher quality.

The "New Mood" represents no single movement, but its power is great.

Reilly told about a Chamber of Commerce in Florida which felt obliged to strike from its literature, first the word "growth" and then, a little later, the word "progress."

Nevertheless, New Mood or no New Mood, we must face this fact: development will continue, even quicken. More households are being formed each year than in the 1960s—one third more. Ahead is a period of construction second only to the boom after World War II.

So, two powerful and uncompromising forces are in motion: the demand for stern controls on development, and the demand for even more building.

Impasse? No, says Reilly. Rather, the New Mood, with its stubborn, sometimes irrational energy, gives us an unparalleled chance to arm ourselves with new methods of directing urban growth while protecting key lands. For the first time, the public is taking plans and planners seriously. It is willing as never before to accept limits on the use of private land.

There are two challenges: first, we must build not only more but also better. New, rebuilt, or expanded communities must be soundly designed and good to live in. Second, we must do much better at preserving things we value: natural land, scenic open space, cultural values, the quality of life. This is the basic demand of New Mooders.

On the development side, the best hope lies in major planned developments on large blocks of land. Diversity, environmental quality, "smallness" can be built in. Communities may discover that the most effective way to encourage good development is not to keep hitting developers over the head with heavier chains but to reward quality in conservation, design or social sensitivity by allowing density bonuses, aiding with sewer hookups, speeding reviews and rezonings. Plans should aim not only to prevent bad development but also to encourage good development. Government should encourage such developments with various subsidies.

As for preservation: government might buy the land it seeks to keep out of development, but Reilly feels strongly that it is best simply to restrict its use under the police power. Only when actual public use is to be made of property is its government purchase necessary. Prime agricultural lands must be protected, and tax relief to an owner who commits himself to keeping his land in production is one way to do that, but it must be coupled with strong long-term assurances against development.

Reilly cautions that the opportunity presented by the rise of the "New Mood" may not last. Today development interests and "New Mooders" alike appear willing to seek answers in the new kinds of land-use planning and control.

But, moods pass and this willingness cannot be counted on to last indefinitely.

___

Alfred E. Heller
San Francisco
Founder, *California Tomorrow*

"Planning," in the public mind, is something government does. And of the outside experts who brought invaluable information to the California Land-Use Task Force, all but one spoke of government planning initiatives and of problems government encounters in attempting to bring order into the use of land.

Alfred Heller, founder of California Tomorrow, a

statewide environmental organization, had a different story to tell: the instructive history of *The California Tomorrow Plan*.[1]

That history began with a government failure. In 1959, the State Legislature ordered work to begin on a state development plan. Ten years and $4 million later, the State Office of Planning produced, says Heller," a turgid document which called for the creation of exactly the thing it should have been itself—a plan for the future of California."

So California Tomorrow put together its own working group to produce a plan of its own., The resulting book, *The California Tomorrow Plan* is more precisely a model for a plan—an attempt to show how statewide planning might proceed.

The working group began with a list of problems facing California, and studied two prototype strategies for solving those problems.

First, we might continue to attack our difficulties one at a time, usually at the point of crisis. This traditional method, the team concluded, had had some successes; but its failures are more than we can afford. Everyone plans, no one coordinates. Single-purpose government agencies—created one after another, crisis by crisis—can only see their narrow version of the public interest. The state budget—maybe the greatest practical determinant of what happens to California—is put together each year in a policy vacuum. Could this haphazard approach bring good results? It has not and cannot, says *The California Tomorrow Plan*. The future we face, if we pursue *ad hoc*, single-purpose solutions to our problems, is bleak; the California Tomorrow team calls that future California One.

Against this background Heller described the possible future called California Two—a California shaped by the coordinated planning reform which *The California Tomorrow Plan* proposes. Some elements of reform:

A system approach. The state planning process (like the CT Plan itself) would begin with a systematic survey of problems, to reveal underlying causes of disorder. To correct these fundamental afflictions, basic or "driving" policies would be developed and adopted. (Heller and Jerry Goldberg, associate of Skidmore, Owings & Merrill, who led the professional staff of *The California Tomorrow Plan*, described in some detail the systematic techniques developed for the Plan.)

A California State Plan. A State Planning Council (appointed by the Governor) would prepare a comprehensive statewide plan. The Legislature would amend and enact it. The state budget each year would be a part of the plan and an expression of it. It would be organized around the state's adopted driving policies. Those policies and some of *The California Tomorrow Plan* components are:

1. Provide political strength:

Government reforms to insure a workable and democratic planning process; the creation of a State Planning Council and regional governments;

the strengthening of local government, including the establishment of community councils.

2. Provide economic strength:

A guaranteed minimum income for the residents of California; strong state and regional building programs; the encouragement of family farming; the creation of a regional system of planning, budgeting, and financing to translate a broad range of public goals into accomplishment.

3. Guide settlement:

A state land use zoning plan; a state infrastructure plan; the creation of amenity standards to guarantee a basic quality of life to every Californian; a state policy on population.

4. Guide resource use:

A statewide program of energy usage; a set of tax policies and regulations designed to encourage the wise use of land and resources.

Regional governments. Multi-purpose regional governments, as noted above, would be established in the 10 planning regions of California. Each would have a directly-elected governing council. They are a key element of *The California Tomorrow Plan*. Regional plans, similar in outline to the state plan but of finer detail, would be adopted and revised yearly. Local governments would continue to carry out most of their current responsibilities within the framework of local and regional plans.

So thorough a reform can come only in stages, and the plan recommends a series of steps which can be taken to bring it about. Smaller innovations than those recommended may work; yet such change is not automatically for the better. In the words of *The California Tomorrow Plan* the test must be: "Is this proposal part of a comprehensive plan for solving problems, and if so, what is the plan and where does the proposal fit it?"

[1]*The California Tomorrow Plan,* published by William Kaufmann, Inc., One First St., Los Altos, Calif., 1972.

Gilbert Finnell
Tallahassee, Florida
Professor of Law, Florida State University
Member, Florida Environmental Land Management
Study Committee
(Visiting Scholar, American Bar Foundation, 1975)

When a state moves for an increased rise in land use planning and regulation, no longer leaving the entire job to local government, there are several different approaches it might take. The Florida legislature in 1972, sought to leave as much authority as possible with local government, intervening only in areas of particular statewide concern or in the cases of certain major proposed developments—an approach modeled after Article 7 of the tentative American Law Institute model code.

In the Florida system there are three main actors: a

State Land Planning Commission which studies and recommends; an *Administration Commission* (consisting of the Governor and 6 elected Cabinet members) which takes action; and *local governments,* which in two limited special cases are bound by Commission guidelines and decisions.

1. Areas of critical state concern. The State may step in to plan the use of areas judged to be of special importance to the people of the state. The State Land Planning Agency suggests possible "critical areas" and development controls which should apply within them. The Administration Commission draws boundaries and enacts guidelines for control. Then the job is handed on to the local governments. Each must submit its own plans to the Commission. If the Commission finds the local plans inadequate, it imposes its own planning controls until new local plans are developed to fit state guidelines.

Also, any local decision in a critical area may be appealed to the Commission. No more than five percent of the land surface of the state may be included at one time in "areas of critical concern."

2. Development of regional impact. Under this provision, local approval of major developments can be appealed to the Governor and Cabinet. The law specifies what developments have "regional impact" and may be so appealed. It also requires one of ten regional agencies (principally existing COG's) to prepare a regional impact of the social and other impacts of the proposal. Again local government makes the initial decision, subject to appeal, but "must consider" the regional impact report and any adopted state plan. (A companion state land planning process was also passed in 1972.)

How has this system worked? In the first year, says Finnell, the laws have been carried out haltingly. In early 1974, the Administration Commission had yet to designate a single "area of critical state concern." (The Florida Legislature, in fact, by-passed the planning process and itself declared the Big Cypress Swamp an area of critical state concern excepting it from the 5 percent restriction.) Also, funding was initially inadequate. Now, however, the Green Swamp has been designated, the Florida Keys are about to be, and funding has improved.

Though frank about these and other problems, Finnell observes that the reform of land-use planning in Florida has only begun. Since 1971, new bills have been introduced and passed each year. Work is going forward on a comprehensive statewide plan and on a state growth policy. The regional agencies are becoming better staffed and assuming an important role.

An interim citizens board organized to make long-range recommendations and help in implementation of the act for the first two years, has issued its final report and made strong recommendations for a stronger local planning process and better wetlands and coastal protection. Finnell's hopes for Florida's planning process are high.

Fred Bosselman
Chicago, Illinois
Attorney-at-Law
Co-author, *The Quiet Revolution in Land-Use Control* and *The Taking Issue*

How far can government restrict the use of private land before restriction becomes confiscation, a "taking"?

The Fifth Amendment to the U.S. Constitution provides: ". . . nor shall private property be taken for public use without just compensation." Frequently the regulation of land-use has been compared to a physical confiscation of property: something government should pay for.

According to Bosselman, the "taking issue" scarcely existed in this country until 1922, when Justice Oliver Wendell Holmes of the Supreme Court defined this rule: "If regulation goes too far, it would be recognized as taking" (Pennsylvania Coal vs. Mahon.)

Since then state courts have been attempting to decide how far is too far. Bosselman identifies three periods in their treatment of the question. Between 1930 and 1960, he sees little definite pattern in state court decisions. Then, in the early 1960s, when the first environmental laws and ordinances were enacted, state courts rather consistently judged these regulations so restrictive that payment was required. Finally, in the late 1960s and in the 1970s, the opposite interpretation has prevailed. Courts have become steadily more willing to sustain regulation without payment, especially when the restriction is based on careful planning or on guidelines set up by regional agencies.

The Supreme Court of California has seemed particularly willing to uphold regulation, even when almost every practical use of a piece of land is ruled out.

At the moment, the legal situation seems rather clear. But the "taking issue" remains enormously important, not as a legal problem, but as a political one. Both landowners and local governments often assume that owners have a more absolute property right than in fact they have; this belief makes local officials cautious in their attempts to control land-use. Compromises are made which may be bad for all sides. The Legislature, too, knowing how seriously land-owners (and voters) take the issue, is slow to act on new planning measures.

What happens next? Among several possible choices, two seem most likely to be made.

First, the matter could be left where it stands. As landowners become reconciled to the legal situation, the issue might become less important.

Second, the state could work out rules by which landowners could receive some compensation not required by present law. In England, government makes some payment to an owner whose land under regulation can no longer provide him "reasonable beneficial use" but there are many exceptions where the governmental purpose is an overriding one. Such a standard might be a reasonable one to use as a starting point for any state that is planning to try such an approach in this country.

In the long run it would produce a much better

result if the "taking issue" were not treated as a constitutional test of what must be done but a legislative test of basic fairness to the public as well as to individuals. The strictness of the regulation should not be as important as its reasonableness.

Thomas P. Gill
Honolulu, Hawaii
Attorney-at-Law
Former Lieutenant Governor of Hawaii

In 1961 Hawaii, first among the states, began to regulate the use of land by statewide zoning.

Under the State Land-Use Law of 1961, as amended, all land in Hawaii is classed into four state zones or "land-use districts." Preliminary zones, based on studies done earlier at the University of Hawaii and existing uses, were imposed in 1961; revised, "permanent" zones followed in 1964; statutory five year boundary reviews were conducted in 1969 and 1974, with piecemeal amendments in the intervening years.

The zoning board is called the State Land-Use Commission. Six of its nine members are appointed by the Governor from Hawaii's six senatorial districts and one at large. The Directors of two state departments— Land and Natural Resources, and Planning and Economic Development—are ex-officio voting members. Only the Commission may alter the boundaries of the four land use districts.

The zones or "districts" are:

An Urban District: Contiguous land in urban use, with enough "reserve area for foreseeable urban growth."

An Agricultural District: Productive crop and range land. Urban type uses essentially prohibited.

A Conservation District: Lands valuable for watershed, wild-life, recreation, other resources. In large part this is state-owned land, closed to most kinds of development.

In 1964, the Legislature added a **Rural District** of mixed agricultural and large-lot (half-acre) residential use. This zone has been criticized as a tool for introducing development into agricultural land.

In each district, some details of land-use are set by agencies other than the Commission. The Conservation District is administered by the State Department of Natural Resources; the Urban Districts are under the authority of the four counties (Hawaii's only local governments); in the Agricultural and Rural Districts control is shared between the counties and the commission. Non-conforming uses may be granted special permits by the controlling agency or agencies.

There have of course been some problems in applying the land-use-law. In some cases there has been conflict and inconsistency. It has been notably difficult to persuade the State Department of Taxation to reassess private property according to the uses permitted by state zoning. There is conflict between county plans and land use zoning. Though mandated by law, there is no effective state general plan.

Despite such difficulties, Gill feels that the Land-Use Law has made a great difference in Hawaii. It has slowed the loss of farm and resource land—losses which the people of these small islands cannot afford. The zones have meant more time for further planning and have tended to restrain urban sprawl. And they have made it easier for Hawaii to control its future.

But a zoning mechanism, or any mechanism, can never be the whole answer to problems of land use. There must be a formal agreement about what uses are proper: a statewide plan. Then zoning, and roads, and public services and utilities, and taxation policies may all be designed to bring about the desired pattern of use.

This coordination has taken place only imperfectly in Hawaii. But, with the land-use zones as an essential first step, it is possible.

Gill concludes that no system of land-use regulation will work until people begin to think of the land as a limited resource belonging to all rather than an expendable commodity. What we lack, says Gill, is "a reverence toward the land."

Gerald Talmadge Horton
Atlanta, Georgia
Member, Georgia House of Representatives

Gerald Horton has made it his business to follow the rapid development of statewide land-use planning across the United States. In his research he has come to several conclusions about what is right with the new methods—and what is wrong with them. He fears that the faults in these new systems will cause the public to react against them.

Some of the faults are:

1. The planning laws being passed today are essentially negative. They regulate, limit, restrict. The command is always "Thou shalt not." This is wrong: a state must know what needs to be accomplished, as well as what needs to be prevented. A state growth and development policy is as important as a state policy for conservation, preservation and protection.

2. Often the new laws are mere mechanisms, guided by no real policy. They control—but nobody knows what principles are to be followed in the control. To be sound, state land-use regulations must grow out of state land-use policies.

3. The new laws seldom establish regional agencies to plan and regulate land-use. Local governments and state government cannot do the whole job: the gap between the levels is too wide. A middle level is required.

4. The new systems commonly fail to regulate the biggest developer of all: government itself. The actions of local, state, and the federal government agencies are not required to conform to land-use plans. Yet some of the biggest land-use decisions are made quietly and irrevocably when money is committed to highways, air-

ports, major educational institutions and other capital improvements. Further, at least half the land in many states is government-owned.

5. The planning systems of local government, regional organizations and the states are seldom comprehensive. That is, they deal with the physical use of the land only, not considering the human problems— education, housing, employment, social services— that are closely tied to land use.

6. Typically the new controls apply to only part of the land of a state: to "critical areas." This, says Horton, won't do. No land is unimportant, and the proper use of part depends on the proper use of all. (He does not argue, however, that all land use should be regulated directly by state authority.)

7. Horton finds the environmental impact analysis a most unsatisfactory tool: "slow, expensive, and picky." He feels that *plans,* rather than individual projects, should go through this kind of analysis.

8. Finally, a very basic and common omission: Legislatures pass bills setting up new methods of planning and control—but do not appropriate the money to make the systems work.

Horton likes to restate his list of negatives as a set of recommendations. A state system of land-use planning and land-use regulation should:

    a. be well-funded
    b. consider all the land
    c. be guided by clear policies
    d. direct the actions of local governments and state agencies
    e. be positive, dealing as much with needed development as with needed preservation of land
    f. be comprehensive, dealing with more than just the physical use of land
    g. part of the work and part of the authority should go to regional government agencies. The responsibility of each level of government should be clear, with each job specifically defined.

Photo credits:

Ansel Adams: top, pg. 58.
Bay Area Rapid Transit District: top right, pg. 69.
Bruce Barnbaum: pp. 2, 56.
Dick Conrat: pp. 41, top 49, 63, left 65, 71, 75, right 80.
Dr. Geoffrey Fricker: pp. 36, 40.
Evan Johnson: pp. 32, 34, 38, 43, 44, 45, 46, 50, 51, 52,
               bottom 58, 66, 68, bottom 69, 70, 72, 74, left 80.
Long Beach Independent Press—Telegram: pg. 79.
Walt Mancini: pp. 35, 57.
Pacific Gas and Electric Company: pp. 62, 64.
David Plowden: pp. 59, 60.
Resources Agency: pg. 54.
Julius Shulman: pp. 42, 48, bottom 49, 81.
Southern California Edison Company: pp. 7, 31.
Southern California Rapid Transit District: top left, pg. 69.
Tom Tracy: pg. 76.
Trend Photography: pp. 6, 7.

INDEX

ABAG, 22ff
Advertising, outdoor, 25
Aeronautics, Division of, 68
Agencies, 14ff, 25ff
Agriculture, 10, 26, 47–53, 74
Air basins, 17, 19, 48
Air pollution, 9, 16ff, 21, 25, 40, 42, 48, 61
Air Pollution Control Board, San Francisco
    Bay Area, 24
Air quality, 8, 13, 17f
Airports, 15, 18, 23, 24, 30
Alameda County, 24
Amenities, 26, 40
Annexation, 30
Apartment houses, 26, 27
Assessments, 29, 35, 37, 73, 78
Automobiles, 17, 18, 33, 40, 61f

Bay Area Rapid Transit System (BART), 24,
    73
Bay Area Conservation and Development
    Commission (BCDC), 14, 19, 24f, 41, 58,
    78
Bay Area Pollution Control District, 24
Bay Area Sewage Services Agency (BASSA),
    24
Bay Delta Resource Recovery Board, 24
Beaches, erosion control, 21, 24f
Birth rates, 39
Bridges, transbay, 24
Budget, 8, 16, 68f, 73f
Building codes, 28, 33–37, 42
Building permits, 28f.
Buses, 67
Business, retail, 34, 37

Cabinet, State, 8, 16
California, Caltrans, 16ff, 68ff;
    Environmental Quality Act of 1970, 41;
    Land Conservation Act, 29; Planning and
    Conservation Foundation, 6, 13n; Tahoe
    Regional Planning Agency (CTRPA), 25;
    Water Plan, 20f; Water Project, 62
Cargo, 67
Census, Bureau of, 12
Chaparral lands, 57
CIR, 8, 14, 16, 21
Cities, 12, 23, 26, 33–37
Citizen participation, 8, 18f, 28, 34ff, 68
City government, 26, 40
Clean Air Act of 1970, 42
Coal, 55
Coastal plans, 21
Coastal Zone, 14, 19, 20, 24, 25, 41, 58, 78

Colleges, community, land acquisition by,
    17
Commuting, 40, 67, 69.
Compensation policies, 8, 77, 79, 80f
Condemnation, 42f
Conservation and Development
    Commission, San Francisco Bay, 58
Conservation, 20, 21, 26, 55
Constitution, California State, 29, 69f, 79, 80
Constitution, United States, 77–81
Construction, 25, 29, 43, 48
Contra Costa County, 24
Convention centers, 24
"Cost-benefit rate", of taxation, 73
Counties, 10, 11, 23ff
County Planning Commission, jurisdiction
    over airports, 30
Crime, 34
Cropland, 10
Crops, 40, 47, 48, 51, 52

Data bank, state-wide, 8
Density, 10, 19, 27f, 40, 61f, 67, 78. See
    also Zoning
Defense, Department of, 12
Desert, 47
Development, 8, 10, 19f, 25ff, 27, 33, 39ff,
    48, 77f, 81
Displaced person, housing for, 34, 37
Due Process, 8, 79

Earthquakes, 26
Ecological reserves, 20
Economic growth, 25f
Education, land-use for, 26; inequalities in,
    74
Electricity, 9, 19ff, 62, 64
Eminent domain, See "Taking"
Emission standards, 18
Employment, 34, 37, 40
Endangered species, 20
Energy, 8, 9, 10, 12, 19f, 31, 34, 40, 48, 55,
    61ff, 67f, 75
"Enforceable restriction," 29
"Entitlement", 29
Environment, 26, 30, 40
Environmental impact report (EIR) 15, 16, 18,
    19f, 23, 29f, 30, 41, 68
Environmental Protection Agency (EPA), 18
Environmental quality, 8, 22
Environmental Quality Act (California,
    1970), 29f, 41
Equalization, of tax support, 74
Exports, U.S. agricultural, 47

Farm workers, 17
Fertilization, 48, 61f
Finance, State Department of, 12
Fire, effect on ecosystems, 56f
Fish and Game, Department of, 14, 20
Flood Control, 23, 25, 48
Food, 9, 29, 47f, 52
Forest land, 10, 48
Forest service, U.S., 12
Fossil fuels, 55, 61
Freeways, 33, 40
Funding, 13, 16, 27f, 36f, 67, 69ff, 70. See
    also Taxation

Gasoline, 40, 62, 67ff
Glass, 55
Gold, 55
Governor, 8, 16, 20, 81
Grants, federal, 23, 28
Growth, 15, 22, 23, 25f, 29, 40ff
Great American Dream, 67

Harbors, 17, 21, 24
Heating, 62
Hemet-Sun City, 39
Highways, 16, 17f, 23ff, 29, 67f
Historical landmarks, 28
Hospitals, 23, 28
Housing Act of 1974, 39
Housing and Urban Development, U.S.
    Department of, 16, 28, 39
Housing Authority, 28f
Housing and Community Development,
    California Department of, 36; Act of
    1974 (U.S.), 36
Housing, findings, 44ff

Improvement Districts, 30
Indian land, 12
Industry, 26
Inner city, 33f, 37, 43
Insurance, 81
Irrigation, 47f

Joint Exercise of Powers Act, 22f

Land, 8, 9, 10, 12, 20, 22, 26, 29, 33, 34,
    40, 57ff; acquisition of, 17, 21, 28, 33,
    37; costs; 40; ownership, 12, 27, 77ff,
    80; public, 22, 57ff, recreational, 20f, 26;
    vacant, 34; values, 73, 78
Land Conservation Act (California), 29
Land Management, Bureau of, 12

Landfill, 25, 55
Lands Commission (California), 14, 22, 57, 59,
Land-use, 9f, 13, 18, 22f, 26, 30, 35, 42, 78, 80; Land-use Council, 8, 81; Land-use legislation, 8, 26ff, 35, 37; Land-use Plan (proposed), 8, Chapter Three
Law, in land-use, 79; Planning, 22
Legislature, 17, 20f, 27f, 68ff, 78ff
Libraries, 24
Livestock, 52, 56
Los Angeles County, 10ff, 70

Marin County, 10f, 24, 49
Mass transit, 16f, 24, 67, 68ff
Metal, 55
Metropolitan Transportation Commission (MTC), 15, 24
Military reservations, 10
Minerals, 55, 73
Minnesota, Twin Cities Metropolitan Area, 73
Minorities, 34, 37, 43
Mobil homes, 25, 39
Mulford-Carrell Air Resources Act (1967), 17

Napa County, 10f, 24, 49
Natural resources, 21f
Navigation, 14, 21
Nevada, 25
New towns, 43f
Noise, 8, 16, 26
Nuclear wastes, 61
Nutrition, 48

Ocean, 21
Office of Planning and Research, 8, 16, 47, 51, 69
Oil, 22, 55, 62
Overgrazing, 56
Oregon, 47, 56
Open space, 9f, 16, 23, 26ff, 33, 39, 41, 51, 55, 58

Parks, 18, 20, 29, 34, 37
Parks and Recreation, Department of, 14, 20
Permits, 14, 18ff, 20, 22, 25, 26, 29f, 41
Pasture, 10
Pension funds, 77
Police power, 23, 25, 28, 77ff
Pollution, 18, 21, 26, 48
Population, 9, 12, 25f, 30, 33, 39, 41f, 55, 61

Private enterprise, 17, 20, 27, 36f, 39, 41ff, 74
Private property, 12, 25f
Proposition 5, 69
Proposition 20, 25
Public health, 77; safety 26
Public interest, 21f
Public Utilities Commission, 19, 22
Public Works Board, 14, 17f

Quality, architectural design, 29
Quarrying, 58

Railroads, 17
Rainfall, 47
Rangeland, 48, 56, 57
Rapid Transit, 24
Reclamation Board, 20
Recreation, 4, 20f, 26, 34, 37
Recycling, 55
Redevelopment, 28
Regional agencies, 15, 22, 23, 25
Relocation, 28
Rent, 39
Reservation Lands, 22
Resources, 8, 9, 18, 20, 46ff, 55ff, 59
Retired persons, 34, 37
Revenue-sharing, 73f
Right-of-way, 24
Rivers, Sacramento and San Joaquin, 20

Sacramento, 23, 42; County, 10f, 49
Sales tax, 73
Salt, 21, 25
San Bernardino County, 10f, 22
San Diego County, 10f, 70
San Francisco, Bay, 19, 25; City and County; 24
San Mateo County, 10f, 24
Santa Clara County, 10f, 24
Schools, 29, 33
Senate, California, 8, 20
Serrano vs. Priest, 74
Sewage treatment, 19, 23, 42
Shopping centers, 18
Slums, 28
Smog, 48, 67
Soil, 25, 47f, 52
Soil Conservation Service, 48
Solano County, 10f, 24
Solar energy, 61
Solid Waste Management Bureau (SWMB), 21, 25, 55f

Sonoma County, 24
Southern California Association of Governments (SCAG), 22f, 67, 70
Southern California Development Guide, 23
Special districts, 13, 23f, 30
Standards of quality, 8
Streets and Highways Code, 26
Strip developments, 40
Subdivisions, 12, 15, 20, 25, 28f
Suburbs, 9, 10f, 28, 39ff, 49, 51, 61f
Supreme Court, California, 78, 80
Sustained Yield, 56

Tahoe Regional Planning Agency (TRPA), 15, 25, 41, 58, 78
"Taking" clause, U.S. Constitution, 28, 77ff
Taxation, 8, 15, 29, 31, 33, 35ff, 42, 48f, 67, 69f, 73f, 80
Technical assistance program (of SCAG), 23
Timber, 25, 47f, 56, 58, 74
Transportation, 16ff, 24, 68ff, 70, 71

Unemployment, 62
Unincorporated areas, 30
University of California, 14, 17, 21f, 47
Urban renewal, 8, 15, 28f, 31, 33ff, 42f, 62, 74
Urbanization, 10, 19, 33f, 37, 40, 47f, 51
U.S. Army Corps of Engineers, 20, 41

Variances, 30
Vehicle exhaust controls, 18
Ventura County, 10f, 49

Waste Management, 18f, 26, 55f
Water, 20, 21, 56; basins, 21; Commission (California), 20; pollution, 8, 13, 18f, 19, 48; Resources, Department of (California), 10, 14, 17, 20f; Resources Control Board, 14, 18ff
Water Pollution Control Act of 1972, 18
Water Project and Aqueduct, 20
Water Quality Control Board, 29
Watershed, 20ff, 25f, 55
Waterways, 25
Wetlands, 25, 58
Wildlife, 20, 55
Williamson Act (1965), 29, 49ff
World War II, 30

Zoning, 15, 16, 25, 27ff, 30, 35ff, 47, 49ff, 78